It's Always a Check Ride

It's Always a Check Ride

TINA MCNEICE

To Greg,
Airplanes!
Aviation!

Enjoy,
Tina McNeice

Deeds Publishing | Athens

Dedicated to

My Dad,
Hayward Stanley Florer, Sr.

Pilot
Safety Expert

Contents

Preface

This is a sort of history book. The events I have written tell about "the good ole days" of Stewardesses and Flight Attendants. Back when we stood at the door of the airplane as the passengers were getting off at their destination and we would fix a man's tie or wipe lipstick off his cheek or lip, tuck in the size or brand label on a blouse or shirt. As a group, we claim the first to wish our passengers, "Have a good day!" But we really meant it, as if with our encouragement, their day would be better.

These are my stories of evacuations, problem passengers, happy, sad, scary, different airplanes and pilots, domestic and international, Vietnam and 9/11. On the airplane there were lots of other Flight Attendants, these are their stories too.

Included are stories about my husband, my parents, and my brother. You will see how they weave into my flying career. I flew with American Airlines for 37 years, from September 17, 1965 to January 1, 2003, based in Buffalo, Washington, D.C., Los Angeles, Dallas, and Miami.

Amazing, just amazing.

Come Fly With Me and see how "It's Always a Check Ride."

Flight 76

This trip originated in Los Angeles (LAX) to Washington's Dulles Airport (IAD), I was 1st Stewardess on a 747, there were a total of twelve Flight Attendants on board with three cockpit crew members, the Captain's name was Bill Cherry. The 747 has four engines, two on each wing.

Before boarding the full load of 366 passengers, the gate agent notified us that we would be pre-boarding a prisoner with a U.S. Marshal and that the Captain had approved the paperwork on the Marshal's gun. The prisoner was an incredibly fat man, in fact so fat he had to be manacled by the waist with a chain to the Marshal as handcuffs couldn't lock around his wrist. They were seated and boarding proceeded normally. We know that prisoners' handcuffs are removed before take-off as everyone has the right to exit in the case of an emergency. Take-off was normal.

After take-off, the Flight Attendant in charge of coach called me in First Class to tell me that the Marshal had come running into the Coach Service Center to say that the prisoner was having a grand mal seizure. She yelled for another Flight Attendant to get the Oxygen as she ran to the prisoner's seat. Our training is not to hold down the patient's tongue with a spoon, but to stand behind the passenger and hold his shoulders close to the seatback to keep the flailing passenger in his seat as best we can. He slumped and passed out right after she got to his seat with the Oxygen. It was the full seizure, he wet himself, almost fell out of his seat, and was unconscious. Thank goodness the Marshal knew this was the real thing. Our Flight Attendants administered Oxygen (O/2), arranged him better in his seat, put a blanket over his lap, and put a cold towel on his head. His neck was so big he had a hard time breathing. One Flight Attendant stayed with him for a while until he woke up and knew where he was.

I went upstairs to the Cockpit to tell Captain Cherry about the prisoner and that he was recovering.

Captain Bill Cherry has quite a notable history, as he was in the Army Air Corp in WWII and was the Captain on the B-17 in 1942 that went down in the Pacific with Eddie Rickenbacker and crew of six. With four life rafts tied together the eight men on board were in the water for 21 days. Bill never spoke of that experience around our crew of Flight Attendants.

We proceeded with the lunch and beverage service. Then, I heard an announcement over the P.A.: "Would a doctor please come to row 28 on the right side of the airplane?" I stopped, had another Flight Attendant take my place in First Class and got to row 28 just as a doctor was approaching the seat on the aisle, and a Flight Attendant arrived with O/2. The man in row 28 was having chest pains. A nurse came to the seat to see if she could assist the doctor. With the Oxygen and having a doctor attending him, the passenger seemed to relax. As he relaxed, he was breath…Over the P.A. (remember, we are still serving lunch) I heard a Flight Attendant ask for a doctor to please come to row 14 on the left side of the airplane. A different doctor was there at the passenger's side in a flash! Again, chest pains, neither of these passengers had eaten, but they both had something to drink, non-alcoholic, but food wasn't the problem. What WAS the problem?

I went upstairs to tell Bill Cherry about our passengers with chest pains.

After the lunch service the movie was showing, but the passengers were a little restless with the medical problems and most didn't even know about the prisoner. Then, in First Class: a woman started screaming, blood curdling, screaming that her husband was losing his pulse. When she started screaming, a First Class Flight Attendant got to her fast, felt his pulse, it was very weak. The other First Class Flight Attendant took the screaming wife away to another seat to quiet her. The husband didn't seem to need Oxygen and with the wife gone he relaxed. The Flight Attendant stayed with him and he drifted off to sleep.

I went to the cockpit to tell Bill.

The prisoner had another seizure, not as bad, but continued the Oxygen.

Now, we have three on Oxygen, and a weak passenger in First Class.

Reports: I started with names, addresses, time of incident, altitude of aircraft at time of incident, witnesses, etc. When ...

BANG! The airplane lurched and knocked me down. I raced up the stairs to the cockpit. The two pilots and the flight engineer were flipping switches, talking on the radio, each busy with his duties. They knew I was there, silent, when Captain Cherry said, "OK, Tina, this is what we've got—engine number two jumped into reverse and we don't know why. We were still on autopilot and we haven't started down into Dulles yet. We have shut number two engine down but we don't know about the others. With all the problems in the cabin, I don't want you to prepare for an emergency landing. We are fine for now, but alert all the Flight Attendants to check their doors to make sure they are clear and usable."

We landed just fine. No further incidents. We were met by fire trucks and several ambulances, but no problems.

There is an addendum to this event. We found out later from Captain Cherry that a week before our flight, an engine on another carrier's 747 had also jumped into reverse with no prior warning and another occurred on a third carrier one week after our problem. Boeing, the FAA, and AA maintenance figured out that these newly designed engines were jumping into reverse at about 300 hours of operation. That's not very long, maybe a little over a month, but the airlines responded quickly and replaced the engines with new or reworked engines and there were no more problems.

As I have relived and fretted about that day in 1970, I think there must have been an imperceptible vibration that no one could have anticipated or measured before that engine went into reverse. Our passengers with marginal medical problems didn't need much to cause an event in their bodies.

Thank goodness for oxygen. Thank goodness for ice and coffee grounds and thank goodness for our incredible training. We use ice on bleeding problems, including with mothers after childbirth, we use dry coffee grounds on our air sickness problems, that is, vomit, and we use oxygen for everything else!

Pre-Flight

The Pilot's Vision

My Dad was a pilot and a safety expert. With my stories, I need to include some of his stories and even some of my Brother's stories.

Let's start by going back to when I was three years old and a Daddy's girl. I didn't have a baby brother yet and I adored my Mother, but my Mom was with me all day. We both lived for my Dad coming home in the evening. On Saturdays, I accompanied him to do all the things that dads do on their days off. I particularly remember going to the hardware store. He chose a hardware store that gave a chocolate chip cookie to children on Saturday mornings.

I told my Mother that I wanted a brother. She said that I would have to ask Jesus. I did. Then I started talking about my baby brother and in a few months, she was pregnant.

I'm smiling as I remember standing behind my Daddy's right shoulder in the front seat of the car while he was driving. I talked a mile a minute telling him about playing with my "Tony Doll," and making a fort in the living room with tables and chairs. While I was talking away in the car, one day I snatched his chin around to face me and I said, "Look at me when I'm talking to you!"

That probably did it for me standing behind his shoulder in the car.

Then I sat in the front seat beside him, as he wouldn't let me stand up on the seat, but from there I couldn't see out. Every time we stopped at a traffic light he put his hand out to hold me in place. Mother did the same, especially if we stopped suddenly.

Then the Pilot's Vision kicked in: I remember him saying to my Mom in 1949: "We should have safety belts in cars, if we have them on airplanes, we should have them in cars too."

Others were coming up with the same thought pattern. Automobile companies did not install safety belts as standard equipment in cars until 1959 and the government didn't require safety belts until 1970.

Note: In "Stew School" we were informed that the name changed from "safety belt" to "seat belt" as the airline industry really started taking off and American Airlines didn't want passengers to think there was a problem with safety. Seat belts became just a matter of fact.

My Dad, Hayward Stanley Florer, Sr., really focused on safety and suffered with every accident, mishap, or problem on any airplane. He lamented: "We have to find out what causes these airplane accidents, we can't prevent accidents if we don't know what is causing them." With his position in the Civil Aeronautics Agency (CAA) Regulations for Flight Standards, he called in aeronautical engineers that worked with the CAA and Hayward gave them the project of a lifetime:

"Come up with a piece of equipment that can monitor and record the performance of all the instruments inside and out of the airplane including the engines from push-back and take off through landing, and engine shutdown. Then design a matching piece of equipment to record everything that is said in the cockpit or any sounds in the cockpit, like an explosion. An explosion might not be in the cockpit, but that sound could be detected and recorded from another part of the airplane."

I have to interrupt here with a "Daddy's Girl" moment.

When my Brother, Stan, was born my Dad took me to work with

him; I was four. He wasn't comfortable with his duty of brushing my hair, so he took me to a beauty parlor to brush my hair and tie the bow on the back of my dress, every morning. He brought along coloring books and my doll. I loved being with him at work.

That was back in the days when Mothers and new born baby brothers were in the hospital for a week or more. On the way home from the hospital I sat in the back seat and my Mother put Stan in my arms. I held him all the way home with Mother beside us.

In 1954, Mother had to go to Memphis, alone, as her Dad was in a very bad car accident. Papa did recover. While she was gone, Dad took Stan, 5, and me, 9, to see the new John Wayne movie, "The High and the Mighty." It was scary but a wonderful event for the three of us. A few years later, Dad gave us flying lessons.

The CAA Aeronautical Engineers came back to Hayward and said this is impossible, we can't get an instrument to survive the impact and fire. Hayward said to keep working on it. Don't give up as you are going to work on this until it is a reality. If you retire, give your work to your replacement. These engineers were not the only ones working on this vision.

A professor of mechanical engineering at The University of Minnesota, James J. Ryan patented the first "Flight Data Recorder" in 1960. The first "Flight Voice Recorder" was patented in 1961 by Edmund A. Boniface, Jr., an aeronautical engineer with Lockheed Aircraft Company. The cockpit recording lasted for 30 minutes then started a new 30-minute recording. Now the recording runs for two hours before the over print of a new recording. If there is something going on in the cockpit that a Captain or Co-Pilot wants to record, with a push of a button, he can keep it recording without an overprint until the flight lands.

These incredible instruments are called "black boxes", except they are actually orange in color so that they can be found more easily. They also emit a beep that can be detected underwater.

The information obtained from these instruments has changed aircraft and engine manufacturing, flight procedures, and details of flying that are unimaginable. I tip my hat and raise my glass to the Engineers whose tenacity gave us this knowledge.

A pilot's age was another safety concern. Well maybe not his age, but his health as he (or she) grew older. What age was too old?

In 1958, my Dad was promoted to Assistant Chief of Regulations for Flight Standards with the FAA. The growing number of private, business, and commercial pilots had to be certificated to qualify for a pilot's license. The license insured that the pilot had the right training and medical checkups, but age was not specified. This needed research.

My Dad did the research in health, mental, physical, stress, and psychological. Note: now anger is being researched as a health issue. Everyone has stress and health ups and downs. Dad focused on medical. At what age do people start taking pills?

My Dad was a pilot, no matter what else he was, he was a pilot. This decision on mandatory age retirement made him pace the floor, because it affected him too. He talked to doctors of all sorts, including the doctors that gave Pilots their physicals and medical certification. He figured out that people start taking pills around age 60, for high blood pressure, anxiety, blood sugar, heart, headaches, and sleep. He didn't want anybody in the cockpit taking pills for anything.

In 1959, the Mandatory Retirement Age was enacted, the law: Age 60.

This was mostly for commercial pilots, but many businesses and private pilots followed these FAA rules and guidelines with age 60 to retire pilots. If a business would leave the age of retirement open, it could mean a company would have to make a determination on a person by person basis.

I'm going to fast forward here to 1970. After lots of "consternation in the camp," the Pilots' Unions, and massive numbers of private and business pilots asked the FAA to reopen the law and look at it again.

My Dad started all over again with his research. Now he was 54 years old and the age of mandatory retirement from flying was upon him. With new research, talking to Doctors and using scientific medical studies, Hayward determined that 60 is the age to retire Pilots. The law was reviewed again several times but stood until 2007.

The new "Mandatory Retirement Age" became 65.

My Dad isn't credited in writing as the one who determined the retirement age for pilots. I think the FAA Administrator has that distinction. But, as in many important research decisions, more than one person does the work.

Easter Parade, Washington D.C. 1949

Grandparents John Walton Cocke (72) & Maude Lindsay Cocke, (64)
Stan (2 months) and Sis (4)

From the Ground Up

As it works out, I've been a stewardess since I was four years old! We were flying on a DC-6 from Memphis to Washington, D.C., my mother, baby brother, and I were returning from a visit with my grandparents who lived in Memphis. On this flight, after the lunch service, the stewardess entertained me by taking me into the galley to show me all the details of the food, trays, coffee containers, water, ice, and cups, ovens, and refrigerator, everything she used for the service. Then, she sat with my mother in the back of the airplane in an area that was rounded with couches like a lounge. My mother let the stewardess hold my brother, Stan, in fact, she gave the stewardess a bottle to feed him. Everybody was happy!

A man across from the galley rang his call button and turned around to see where the stewardess was, then waved his hand, never mind when he saw that she was busy with my brother. But, I ran to him to ask him what he wanted, he said, "It's not important, I just wanted a cup of coffee." I said, "I can't get you coffee, but I can get some water for you." And, I did. When I gave him the water, I was standing in the aisle, he put his arm around me and said, "I want you to promise me that you will be an American Airlines Stewardess when you grow up." That was in 1950.

I will always wonder if that was "Mister C.R." Smith, founder, president and CEO of American Airlines. I couldn't let him down; I promised.

My Dad was from Oklahoma. His dad, Benjamin, was a high school principal and his mother, Jesse, was the Social Services Director for Osage County. They retired to Benjamin's old family farm established in the Cherokee Strip Land Rush of 1893.

After graduating from Oklahoma's Central State University as a double music major in voice and instrument, Dad taught high school band and choir. On his days off from teaching, he took flying lessons.

As you may have guessed, when the war started, my dad joined the Army Air Corp and was made a Lieutenant flying several types of aircraft. He was based with the Fourth Ferrying Group in Memphis, Tennessee, where he transported fighters and bombers to Europe, Africa, and the Far East. My parents met at a party in Memphis.

My Mother was born in Birmingham, Alabama, raised in Memphis, attended Ole Miss (University of Mississippi) as a journalism major. Then a tragedy happened in her family and her father had to bring both of his girls home from college. Mother's sister, Elizabeth, was going to University of Mississippi for Women (this school was known as: "The W"). My Mother became a teller in a bank in downtown Memphis.

The tragedy was with Mother's older (12 years older) brother, John, and his wife, Emolyn, who were in a terrible automobile accident in Lakeland, Florida. Uncle John's wife was killed and Uncle John required extensive surgery and a steel plate was put in his head. John and Emolyn were in the car with the movie star, Frances Langford who was not seriously injured. But, Uncle John and his children, Fred and Emolyn, had to move to Memphis and live with his parents.

I have to tell you about my Grandfather. John Walton Cocke, born and raised in Alabama. He was the youngest millionaire in Birmingham until the depression hit. He had at least two businesses in Birmingham: Nehi Bottling Company and a Firestone tire store that included a couple of motorcycles with side cars to go change tires. The businesses were very successful. Then he lost everything.

"Papa" didn't waste any time in finding a new job; he sold syrup for Anheuser Busch. It was called "Bud Syrup," before any of their beer was called Bud. Papa sold syrup all over the South. He had many family members to support: His wife Maude, daughters, Amelia and Elizabeth ("Mimi" and "Libby"), his maiden aunt, Amelia Webb, his mother-in-law, Elizabeth Lindsay, and now John, Emolyn, and Fred. And, he was paying the taxes on their old family plantation in Alabama, "Strawberry Hill" in Eutaw.

Papa was very successful selling syrup for Anheuser Busch and Anheuser Busch took very good care of Papa.

About the night my parents met: my Mother told me that when she saw my Dad coming up the walk (in uniform), she said to herself, "There he is, that's the one." They were married three months later, on August 21, 1943.

After flying with the "Fourth Ferrying Group" they were transferred to Miami where my Dad was attached to "Fireball Express," ferrying airplanes into and out of war zones, mostly flying to Europe and North Africa, moving broken airplanes and bringing some back to the U.S. to have major overhauls.

I was born while they were based in Miami, in a famous hotel, The Biltmore, that had been a resort since 1926. During World War II the resort was made into a hospital. I was born in Coral Gables in the "Biltmore Army Hospital" in August of 1945. The Biltmore is still a famous resort with its 18 hole championship golf course and a swimming pool that is the largest hotel pool in the country.

When the War was over, my Dad wanted to be a pilot for American Airlines, but American wasn't hiring. He didn't want to fly for any other airline, so he applied to the Civil Aeronautics Agency (CAA).

He was hired right away and sent to New York's LaGuardia Airport. He worked out of LaGuardia for two years. Then he was transferred to Washington, D.C. and worked out of National Airport at the Regional Office for the CAA, in those old red brick buildings.

There is an interesting story about the move to the D.C. area and my Dad's new job. They sent him to be based in the cupola on the roof of Mt. Vernon, George Washington's estate South of Alexandria, Virginia.

His job was to monitor the vibration airplanes made on Mt. Vernon as they approached National Airport. He had several instruments to measure the impact the vibrations could cause. Mt. Vernon is facing the Potomac River and more and more flights made their approach northbound up the Potomac. The government wanted to make sure that the increasing airline traffic didn't damage Mt. Vernon in any way. He was located in the copula for several months and my Mother and I visited him there a few times. I was two and a half, certainly walking, and there were not very many people around, including guards, so Mother watched me like a hawk.

On one occasion time got away from her while talking to a tour guide; she panicked trying to find me, and she did find me asleep on Martha Washington's bed. In her room, there were steps up to the bed and it must have looked very inviting to me.

Tina, 4, Arlington, Virginia

The Invitation

I consider myself raised in Alexandria, Virginia, but after the fourth grade we moved to Houston, Texas. On the way to Houston, our family drove to Miami in order for my Dad to become qualified on the Boeing-707. It was such a fun Summer for us and so different, we stayed in a hotel close to the beach and enjoyed all that Miami Beach had to offer. I am sure we were there for a month. Dad's training was with Pan Am Flight Training attached to their headquarters in Miami.

Then we were off to Houston where my Dad was the FAA (Changed from Civil to Federal) man in charge of the Houston Airport, now Houston's Hobby Airport. We were there for three years. I remember one time our family was going out to dinner but first we had to go look for and find someone who was flying his kite too high, near the airport. We found him and Dad told him he was in violation, "Take the kite down." Note: Today they probably look for drones.

After Houston, Dad received a promotion to the Regional Office in Ft. Worth. We lived in Ft. Worth for a year and a half.

The next move was back to Washington, D.C. where he became the Assistant Chief of Regulations for Flight Standards. He didn't accept any more moves or promotions so that I could attend all four years in the same high school and the same for Stan, in fact, they stayed in the same house, south of Mt. Vernon estate, until after Stan graduated from West Point.

My high school's graduation ceremonies were held in The Daughters of the American Revolution's Constitution Hall in Washington, D.C. I was in the Mt. Vernon High School Chorus and sang "The Battle Hymn of the Republic" my sophomore, junior, and senior years in that hallowed concert hall. Note: Using my mother's research, family genealogy and DAR national number, I qualified for and joined the DAR in 1984.

After graduation, I was off to college: St. Andrews Presbyterian College (now St. Andrews University), Laurinburg, North Carolina. St. Andrews was a small, four-year, co-ed college. I was interested in early childhood psychology, so I was studying to be an elementary school teacher. What I really wanted to do was to fly! My Dad had given my brother and me flying lessons in a twin-engine Beech craft and a tri-pacer. These days I would have had the goal of being pilot, but that was just about unheard of in the early '60's.

So, I decided, I'll apply to American Airlines (I only wanted American Airlines). If they didn't hire me because I was too skinny or something, I would be a great elementary school teacher or child psychologist.

I wrote American asking what would give me the best chance to become a stewardess for American Airlines. They said that I could apply within three months of my 20th birthday. They said to interview with another carrier to get some experience as the face-to-face interview is the most important thing in being accepted. I did!

Eastern Airlines interviewed me in a hotel near Washington National Airport, in a bedroom! The interviewer sat on one bed facing me sitting on the other bed. I was 19 years old, this guy was probably 30; I was so uncomfortable. I asked him about where Eastern Airlines had bases and what airplanes they flew, then I got out of there.

American Airlines sent me an invitation to interview in an office building in downtown Washington, D.C. Of course, I was so impressed. I bought a new dress, my family drove me to the interview, and I was early. Early enough that the girl (we were only girls in 1965, excuse me, they called us "young ladies") scheduled for her interview before mine wasn't there yet. They interviewed me early. I say "they" as the lady at the desk was probably part of the interviewing team. In my case, no one was waiting for her turn to meet the interviewer.

When there are several young ladies waiting their turn, the lady at the desk surreptitiously observes them. She watches to see if someone chooses to sit alone and doesn't visit with the others waiting to be called in to the interview. American Airlines wants stewardesses who can easily talk to strangers. The interview really starts in the waiting area.

After my interview, our family went out to dinner in D.C. to celebrate. If I had been older, I would have had a drink!

A few details of the interview: Mr. Kistler asked me my name, age, my height, and weight. He looked at my forearms (for scars and dark hair), he looked at my legs from the knees down (for scars). These days they probably look for tattoos. Next, I had to read from a podium, it was a "Taxi-away" Public Address Announcement (P.A.), I guess to hear if I had a whiney voice. He asked me why I wanted to be a stewardess, I told him I wanted to fly on different kinds of airplanes, travel, and meet people. Then he told me the locations of American's bases. He asked if I would relocate to another base if Washington was not available (I said yes). Did I have any questions?

I only asked about the AA Union. Being raised in a "management" family; I didn't know anything about a Union. He said the Union was a "closed shop." Meaning that I was required to be a Union member, I said OK.

Four days later, I received a telegram that I had been accepted pending a medical exam in New York's LaGuardia Airport by an American Airlines medical doctor, that would include hearing and eye tests.

They sent me a ticket to New York, I passed the physical and was cleared to start training at the American Airlines Stewardess College in Ft. Worth, Texas, August 9, 1965. Ten days before my 20th birthday.

Stew School

I reported early to Class 65-14, August 9, 1965, at the American Airlines Stewardess College in Ft. Worth, Texas. I hoped that the class seniority was determined by the time you arrived at the school, but found out it was determined by birth date. Out of our class of 50 from all over the country, I was last.

They weighed us, then measured our height. Well, okay, I expected that within a day or two, but not in the first five minutes. I weighted 84 pounds and was 5 feet 2 and a half inches tall. The instructor said, "You realize that you have to weigh 102 pounds to graduate, don't you?" I said, "I understand."

Once the members of our class all signed in, we assembled in a classroom and the instructor passed out a document for us to sign: 1. I am not married. 2. I would not be married as long as I was employed by American Airlines as a stewardess. 3. I would not have a baby as long as I was employed by American Airlines as a stewardess. 4. I would retire before I turned 32 years of age.

All of this changed with the Equal Rights Amendment.

We started our training with name association. This is when we stood up and said our name, where we were from, and something about us. We were prompted to say something funny or unusual to help an association with our name and face. It was a fun class and must have worked as within two days we really knew everyone's name and some where they were from.

I will say that the President and CEO of American Airlines, Mr. C. R. Smith, emphasized this quality of remembering names. If you met him once, he could say your name even in some distant airport, he was amazing.

Three lady instructors taught this name association class. Then, like a modern day "flash mob" they started singing:

Tripping down the aisle with tray in hand
Here's your coffee, catch it if you can
Pardon me ladies and gentlemen if you all turn blue
I forgot to turn the O2 on for you.
I rang the cockpit 4 times, yes, just 4,
And he came roaring through the cockpit door
I only wanted to know the time of day,
And he reacted in the most undignified way.
They may tell you that their business has gone bankrupt
They may tell you that they've lost their wife and child
They may tell you that the whole darn world's a-gin 'um
And you stand there and you smile, smile, smile.

We all laughed, the song broke the ice and tense feelings we had been trying to hide. These "flash mobs" showed up at different times and no one could figure out when they would occur. They made our training fun.

We learned how to sit, stand, put on coats, get in and out of a car, walk up and down stairs, how to smoke; they didn't want us to smoke, but if we did, they wanted us to know how to smoke like a lady. To smoke like a lady: only smoke when you are sitting down. If you smoke at a party standing up, you have to have a drink in your hand, and don't flick ashes, roll the cigarette in an ashtray. We learned how to put on makeup, heat baby bottles, defuse angry passengers, make announcements over the P.A. We practiced serving trays to each other with the chairs in the classroom lined up like an airplane. We learned to hold the trays in front of us with one above the other, not side by side as they would not fit down the aisle side by side.

Maintenance gave us a big presentation as American wanted us to be confident in our airplanes and equipment. The maintenance man explained to us, among other things, about the "bells" on the airplane as a means of communication. Of course, there is the passenger call bell and the light that is at each passenger's seat. Then there is the means for the cockpit to call us and for us to call the cockpit and each other with two dings. If the cockpit wants us to come to the cockpit, they ding three times. If the cockpit rings four times, it means, drop everything, and come up here right now! I only heard four bells twice in 37 years! Both times were about expected turbulence. We used to be able to call the cockpit with those bells, in the same way, but they can't come out of the cockpit any more.

Here's a funny:

In order to teach us how to remember the color of the lights on the tip of the wings on all airplanes, they said, "the Captain sits on the left side of the cockpit, the light on the left side is red, the Captain is usually old and married: red light, Stop. The co-pilot sits on the right side, he is usually young and single, the light on the right side is green, Go!" The lights haven't changed but times have. You noticed that I never forgot the color of the lights on the wing tips.

A man without an AA girl
Is like a ship without a sail
A plane without a rudder
A jet without a tail

A man without an AA girl
Is like a clock without a hand
But the saddest thing in the whole wide world
Is an AA girl without a man!

Medical and Emergency Procedure Training went on for weeks. The total training school was six weeks. We had to qualify on several airplanes at Stew School, but not all bases flew every aircraft type. Each airplane type had to be certificated to be able to evacuate a full load of passengers using only half the number of exit doors in 90 seconds. Our class qualified on the Boeing 707, the Convair 990, the Convair 880, and the Boeing 727.

Flight numbers, we learned that the last digit of a flight number indicates whether the flight is east or west bound. East bound numbers are even, west bound are odd. North and south depend on if they are slightly east or west bound.

American had sent a booklet to each of us at home before training to start learning the Airport City Codes of all the airports that American served. We also had to learn the mail routes! Amazing, some of the things we don't even think of today. There were only three major cross-country mail-routes back then. When we were first tested on our city code knowledge, we were given a United States map to fill in the names of the states and capitols if we knew them. The instructor didn't collect the test on the states and capitols, but they wanted us to be aware and check ourselves.

A group of instructors started this song outside the classroom and down the hall, but we could hear them singing and coming our way.

A-merican Airlines, A-merican Airlines
A-merican Airlines, A-merican Airlines
We are the girls who fly for American

We like to fly because it's American
We've got looks, we've got charms
We've got two lovin' arms
Many a man has asked for our hand
But, we are the girls who fly for
A-merican Airlines, A-merican Airlines
AA

All this time the instructors were evaluating us on our "outgoing, friendly, co-operative, enthusiastic, easy going dispositions and sincere smiles." Many in the class had weight issues, including me. I needed to gain weight, others had to lose, but we dealt with it. Some worked on exercises as a group, including the one when you sit down on the floor, in this case the hallway of our dorm rooms, and while seated scoot one leg and hip in front of the other with foot flexed, arms straight out parallel to the floor. If you could have seen 40 young ladies, trying to work off pounds and inches, lining the hallway one in front of the other, moving down the hall, across the end and back up the other side, you would laugh until you cried. Sometimes they sang the new songs we had learned from our Flash Mobs! I couldn't join them as I needed to gain weight. Many walked or jogged around the campus in the evening. We had six weeks to accomplish our weight goals. An instructor weighed us every three days to watch our progress. Then, my instructor called me in to say that I was getting chubby cheeks.

She weighed me and I was 98 pounds. Chubby Cheeks? She said that I had to stop gaining. I asked, "What about the requirement that I have to weigh 102 pounds to graduate?" She said that they were waiving that for me. Oh! No! I was "on a roll!" Checking myself almost every day, I finally got up to 102 pounds, I had my instructor check it. She said, "Great, I will write that in your file, now go back down to 98 pounds and stay there."

Yes, weight back then was a big deal. Only over time, and age, did this become a "bigger and bigger" issue. Some of the requirements were relaxed and adjusted as we added another component to our ranks: MEN.

When American started hiring men, the height requirement went from a maximum of 5' 10" to 6' 1"! And we had to have our weight, "in proportion to our height!"

Details: there was a little "consternation in the camp" when they hired men, as each man had a room to himself, women (we changed from young ladies) had to share a room, both in training and on "the line!" So, at the lay-over city, like the pilots, guys got a room by themselves. Even if there were two male F/As, they had separate rooms. We might have had 15 years' seniority, we shared a room, and this guy got a room by himself his first night! This changed, but I think it took two contracts, three years each, and changed about 1976.

Another detail: We were called "Stewardess" until American hired men to fly in the cabin, they didn't want to be called "Steward," that is when we all became "Flight Attendants."

Our uniform was tailor made for each of us by the New York tailor Hart, Schaffner, and Marx, we had three fittings. The uniform included: a light blue 2-piece suit in the Summer (Navy blue in the Winter), a white blouse with pearl buttons and a "fly-boy" collar, a full slip, girdle, hook up stockings, a coat, hat, scarf, a serving smock (we only wore when the flight was over an hour and a half), Navy blue heels and flats, a suitcase, and white gloves. We were required to wear red nail polish, mascara, (no eyeliner, no eye shadow), some pink blush, and red lipstick. Our hair had to be two inches above our collar. We were required to have our up-to-date manual with us on every trip and have a working flashlight and watch. These things were checked on every check ride.

There were 48 of us to graduate when graduation day finally arrived, our class had lost two students, both went home to get married. An instructor read out the choices of our base assignments (in our interview we said that we would go anywhere). They were: New York City, San Francisco, Dallas, and Buffalo. These were awarded according to our class seniority, so the bottom sixteen of our class had no choice, we went to Buffalo.

On September 17, 1965, it was 93 degrees in Ft. Worth, Texas, when we arrived in Buffalo it was 63 degrees!

Gradution day, September 17, 1965
American Airlines Stewardess College, Ft. Worth, Texas

Graduation class 65–14

Tina is on railing 7 down from top

Buffalo

Indoctrination

Indoctrination at our Buffalo base was a briefing from our supervisor which included: where to sign-in before each trip, how and where to meet the Captain, when and what airplanes we need to qualify on, and places available to live near the airport.

I wanted to qualify on the DC-6 as soon as possible in order to work Buffalo's only trip to Washington, D.C. and maybe see my family. I also needed to qualify on the Lockheed Electra. As a base, Buffalo mostly flew to cities in the Northeast. We didn't have any non-stops to the west coast.

The most important detail of our indoctrination was to find out about our "first trip!" The supervisor yielded to the manager of our base who introduced herself and began to call out our names in order of seniority (I'm getting used to this by now). She gave the flight number, sign-in time, departure time, airplane type, layover destination, and the time the trip arrived back in Buffalo. There were 16 of us so this took a while, I knew I was last, but, she didn't call my name. She went on about being on time and ordering taxis for our first trip, but she didn't call my name! I raised my hand and said, "You didn't call my name!?" With a slight smile, she said, "What is your name?" When I said, "Tina Florer," she said, as if she was looking up my name, "Let's see, Tina, tonight you are going to New York City, stay at the Commodore

Hotel and tomorrow you are going to have a screen test with Gene Kelly."

What!!?

What about my first trip?

Gene Kelly, the star in "Singing in the Rain!?" In New York City!? Why me?

Gene Kelly planned to make a "Special" on New York City called, "New York, New York." His flight into New York was going to be on American Airlines. There were no jet bridges so a mobile staircase was to be wheeled up to the airplane. When the door of the airplane opened, a stewardess was going to be standing next to Gene Kelly in the doorway of the plane.

Welcome to New York!

Gene Kelly was 5'8," his promoters and directors didn't want a 5'10" stewardess to stand next to him. So, for the screen test, American brought every American Airlines stewardess from all over the country who was 5'3" and under to New York City. The screen test took place in a ballroom, we didn't meet Gene Kelly; each of us walked on the arm of a man Gene Kelly's size. I was not selected, but it was so exciting and an incredible experience. Now I can fly!

To help with expenses five of us from our class found a "duplex" not far from the Buffalo Airport. None of us had a car so we took taxis at all hours to the airport, or to the grocery store. We weren't at "home" together very often but it was nice to have friends to come home to.

My first trip was a Chicago (ORD) turn-around on a Boeing 727. When I got on board the airplane with my new uniform, white gloves, and big smile, the other stewardesses were excited too. When the three pilots came on the plane the 1st Stewardess told them it was my first trip. They were all smiles and glad to meet me. Well, no one had briefed me about the cockpit's indoctrination for new stewardesses: the Flight Engineer, the youngest and newest pilot, put his suitcase down, picked me up and put me in the overhead rack! This is long before there were covers or doors on the rack, just a shelf, and of course, I was little, he didn't need any help putting me up there. Then, they all stood back and watched me climb out, new uniform, girdle, hook up stockings, hat, gloves, and all. I had to get one foot down onto the top of a seat back, then the other, then onto my knees on the seatback and down into the seat. It was all in fun and a big surprise for me.

Then we boarded my first passengers, I stood at the front door with my white gloves and glowing smile. My position was number 3, which meant that I worked in coach and I was not in charge of taking names before take-off. I sat on the front jump seat, next to the 1st Stewardess for take-off and landing. I learned (the hard way) that the 1st Stewardess started a new pot of coffee just before we sat down so that the coffee would be ready and hot when the breakfast service started right after take-off. The first thing I did when I stood up was pull the coffee pot out of the coffee maker, something I hadn't done before and I thought it was going to be hard to pull out. It wasn't. It was full of hot coffee that flew all over my brand- new uniform and down the front of my fly-boy collar and arm. I was mortified.

The 1st Stewardess didn't say much, she just gave me a napkin full of ice and said to sit on the jump seat. The jump seat was out of sight of the First Class passengers. She told me to put ice on me and my uniform, when that melted get more ice and stay out of the way. That was the first leg of my first trip. I will say that while sitting on the jump seat, I took her list of names of First Class passengers and learned them, when they were deplaning, I said goodbye to them by name. Big deal, I had been useless.

We were on the ground in Chicago for two hours then I worked very hard, as trained, back to Buffalo, with no problems. And surprisingly, my uniform showed no sign of the coffee, no signs, ice works. My skin was red for a few days and was an interesting reminder of my first trip.

My next trip was to Washington, D.C. on the DC-6. That plane was like an old friend as I had flown on a DC-6 several times when I was growing up. Think about how times have changed: When my Mother came to National Airport to see me, she not only came to the gate, I was able to bring her on board the airplane with the sandwiches she had brought for our lunch. It was a short visit but such a wonderful moment when she saw me in my uniform for the first time. She got to meet the crew before she went home and then we flew to New York City's LaGuardia Airport and spent the night downtown in the Commodore Hotel.

This is so glamorous.

Every trip was an adventure. I say "adventure" as there were new places that I had never been before, the passengers were so interesting; some had different accents, most were businessmen, some families, many had never flown before.

We learned in Stew School that only 3% of the population in America had ever flown. American Airlines wanted to change that. I am talking about 1965, most people, even business travelers, drove to wherever they were going. As more businesses branched out, the car rental business kicked in and everything changed. It was so interesting to talk to our business travelers. Sometimes businessmen brought their wives with them. Then, through research, we found out that it was the wives or secretaries who chose which airline company the businessman would use.

It was very interesting being based in Buffalo. I found that I didn't really have a winter coat. Virginia coats are not the same, so I bought a warm winter (non-uniform) coat in New York City at Hart Schaffner and Marx who also fitted and made our uniforms.

Snow was amazing. Gas stations made tunnels up to the pumps.

There were walls of snow down the streets. I often walked to the grocery store, but I had to watch how much I bought as two bags were hard to manage walking back with the snow past my knees. I would leave one bag in the snow, go back and get the other, then leap-frog the bags forward to the duplex, with maybe hot chocolate as a reward.

September 29, 1965 in Washington D.C.

AA FORM C110E	*AMERICAN AIRLINES, INC*
TO _____ *Pat & Tina*	**AVOID ORAL INSTRUCTIONS**
SUBJECT _____ *CBS - Special Assignment*	USE FOR PENCIL MEMOS — FOR SHORT RUSH NOTES TO CONFIRM ORAL INSTRUCTIONS — SAVE DICTATION AND TYPING TIME

DATE _____

☐ FOR YOUR INFORMATION   ☐ PLEASE TAKE UP WITH ME
☐ NOTE AND RETURN WITH COMMENTS   ☐ FOR YOUR APPROVAL
☐ PLEASE HANDLE AS REQUIRED   ☐ PLEASE FILE
☐ PER PHONE CONVERSATION   ☐ PLEASE PHONE ME

You are to depart tonight at 9:00 P.M. on Flt. 328 for New York

Your hotel accommodations are at the Hotel Commodore under the name

of Barbara Conway. If you have any problems request to speak with

Mr. Dick Bishop at the Hotel. You are to report in uniform to CBS

Studios on 57th street and 10th Avenue not later than 10:25 A.M.

Report to rehersal Hall # 1. After the rehearsal check available

flight back to BUF and you are expected to return to Base by tomorrow

evening. Claim expenses on Weekly expense statement and be sure to

obtain hotel receipt and retain flight cupon. Submit expense statement

PRINTED IN U.S.A.   *to me.*   *BettyKleiman*

SIGNED _____   STA. _____

Official notification of Special Assignment Screen test with Gene Kelly

A Check Ride?

A check ride was and still is an evaluation or observation by the Stew-ardess' home base supervisor to make sure procedures were being followed. The supervisor sat in a passenger seat in the cabin where her Stewardess was working and watched the service proceed. Some of these procedures were: checking seat belts and items around a passenger's seat, taking and using names in First Class, hanging up a suit coat or sports coat, not holding a glass or cup by the top, only around the side, accompanying a beverage with a napkin, wearing her name tag. Details, and they go on and on, but they were/are important. At some point during the check ride, usually at the end, the supervisor will check required equipment:

1. Flashlight
2. A working watch
3. Cockpit Key (now this key only unlocks the defibrillator)
4. Key to operations area in the airport
5. Up-to-date manual (my first manual only had cabin procedures, later manuals had emergency procedures and location of emergency equipment). Now it's on their cell phones!

Many things about a check ride haven't changed:

Sometimes the Flight Attendant doesn't know she or he is having a check ride, this is called a "blind ride" or "ghost ride." The supervisor giving this ride is from a different base. We are also always aware that a supervisor or executive from another airline may "check our service" at any time and we wouldn't know it.

Of course, our supervisors can't evaluate our emergency procedures on the airplane, but we have to be at "peak of performance" every minute when it comes to emergencies. We have Emergency Procedure Training (EPTs) each year in Ft. Worth at Flagship University, the name changed from American Airlines Stewardess College. We have simulators for every kind of airplane American Airlines has in its system. We no longer line up chairs in a classroom to look like an airplane. Our Flight Attendant simulators are for us to practice arming and disarming the emergency (exit) doors (this means that we attach the slide to the door so that it is not just an entry door with a jet bridge attached), we slide down the emergency slide, we practice with oxygen, both the oxygen bottle that we can carry to a passenger's seat in the event of a medical problem and the oxygen with the mask that is above every passenger seat, smoke in the cabin, two kinds of fire extinguishers: water and chemical, medical equipment, defibrillators, CPR, first aid, pressure on bleeding sites, or ice on bleeding sites, and we practice putting on a life vest, and birthing babies. Our training center has a swimming pool to practice water ditching which is getting out of an exit using the slide as a life raft, we also have life rafts packed in the ceiling of some "over water equipped" aircraft and we practice getting them out of the ceiling with the help of a passenger (Flight Attendant during training).

In writing these procedures down that we requalify on every year, it seems like just an item on a list, but oh, the work and effort that is put into this incredible training is award winning, and it shows.

On one of my first Check Rides when I was based in Buffalo, the only thing the report said was that I had wispy hair. On another check ride out of Buffalo, within my first year, a supervisor pinched my bottom! She said, "You don't have your girdle on." I said, "I don't need a girdle, I weigh 98 pounds and when I hook up my stockings the girdle comes down." She said, "It's required." I said, "I understand." I wore my girdle.

A note here: A girdle gave a smooth, slimming look for a uniform skirt, especially for those who carried a little more weight.

Now, about the Pilots! Oh, Lord, do they have check rides!

A couple, who are long standing friends of mine, are a retired Pilot and Flight Attendant. She has been a friend for almost 40 years, we were based together in Los Angeles (LAX), Dallas (DFW), and Miami (MIA), the last two bases while we were flying International. She met her Pilot when he was our Co-Pilot flying our Boeing 747 SP from Dallas to Tokyo, Japan.

I asked him about Pilot check rides and he says it so well, I will quote his e-mail response:

"Re: check rides. We had two types, those in the simulators, and those on-the-line. After we demonstrated proficiency in flying procedurally normal events like instrument approaches in all kinds of weather, the simulator check rides were more about dealing with abnormal and emergency procedures, like hydraulic/electrical/flight control failures and engine failures and fires. Stuff we couldn't practice in the airplane. What fun.

"The 'line checks' were more about the real world. Prior to departure, we always had to produce our current FAA First Class Medical Certificate which had to be renewed every six months. Without those, we couldn't even leave the gate. And sometimes, a guy would forget to have his licenses with him or would have an expired medical. Dumb and Dumber.

"Occasionally, we also had to show that our publications (with revisions) were up to date in our kit-bags. Usually, just by signing for the airplane and signing the 'release' was the way we signified that we were ready in all respects to go flying. And that we had everything required including licenses, medical, flashlight, publications, etc.

"We always operated as a crew, to emphasize the 'crew concept' and 'standardization.' That is, they could put me in a simulator or an airplane with anyone else in the system, no matter where he or she was based, and we would expect that the other pilot crew member would do exactly as they had been taught, exactly as I had been taught, react exactly as we had been told that we could expect, and vice versa. When we were in the simulator, it would be me (Captain) and a First Officer, training first with a Simulator Instructor, then with a Check Airman/ FAA Designee to give us both the simultaneous check ride. Very rarely would one of us pass and the other fail. We were in it together."

Here's a story about my Dad:

My dad was a Pilot in WWII, then after the war he got a job with the CAA (Civil Aeronautics Agency) which became the FAA (Federal Aviation Administration). Among other jobs, he at one point gave check rides to Pilots who were based in Washington (DCA). To be qualified and keep all his qualifications on the different aircrafts that he was giving check rides, he had checks on himself. I remember one occasion when my mother took my brother and me to National Airport to pick Dad up after work, we were real young, maybe I was six and my brother was two. Mother was directed to where my Dad was: in a "Link Trainer." This was a machine that looked like a big bullet. It was a working cockpit on a wired stand, a simulator. It was used to simulate emergency situations and the Pilot had to deal with them. When this machine stopped its gyrations, my Dad lifted the "hood," saw us standing there and said to my Mother, "Get the children out of here for a while, let me recover." I will never forget the way my father looked, he was sweating and his eyes were bloodshot, he never spoke about it to us, we didn't ask.

On another occasion, my Dad was giving a check ride to a crew based in Washington on a DC-6, which is a four-engine prop (not jet, propellers). My Dad was by-the-book because he wanted only the highest performance from the Pilots he checked and put his name on their ride, but he was a good guy and easy to be around, he was the choir director in our church, a leader...and he didn't "set you up." During this check ride my Dad dropped his pencil. It was dark so he asked the co-pilot to shine his flashlight on the floor of the cockpit, the co-pilot couldn't find his flashlight. Dad said, OK, the Flight Engineer can shine his flashlight over here, he didn't have his flashlight. "Captain, would you hand me your flashlight so I can find my pencil?" No flashlights in the cockpit.

Dad said, "Call the Stewardess, we'll get her flashlight." No flashlight.

At the end of the check ride by the CAA, Dad said, "When I get to work in the morning, I want to see four flashlights on my desk." And, they were, with all four crew members, in uniform.

New story: Finally, I was old enough to learn how to drive, we lived in Texas at the time. My Dad and occasionally my Mother would let me drive short distances and in parking lots. Dad would say when you drive at night don't look at the headlights of the oncoming car, look at the side of the road in front of you until the oncoming car passes. And, don't drive so fast that when you stop, your passengers lean forward.

Safety belts were not required yet. After a few "lessons" my Dad told me to get in the car, this was going to be a "check ride." He did the same procedure with my Brother a few years later. Then, when we were grown, Dad said, "If I'm in the car, It's Always a Check Ride."

Washington,

Washington, D.C

In September 1966 I transferred to Washington's National Airport.
My family welcomed me to live at home with them south of Alexandria near Mt. Vernon. It was wonderful being at home again. Somehow, I needed the security of the love surrounding our family unit. But I mostly wanted to be home for my brother's senior year in high school. My brother was a leader and president of his senior class. Actually, he had been with his class since elementary school. Then during high school he was their freshman class president, sophomore year: school treasurer, junior year: class president.

When the day came for his Class in 1967 to graduate, he gave the speech, the Senior Class President's speech. Mt. Vernon High School has its graduation ceremonies in the DAR Constitution Hall in downtown Washington, D.C. There he was on the stage, talking to his class, about past, present, and future. Oh, there wasn't a dry eye in the house!

My Brother has an incredible singing voice. Of note (!), he was in the Texas Boys Choir in Ft. Worth, when we lived there. He also sang "The Battle Hymn of the Republic" all four years in Constitution Hall in the high school chorus. And, he had a musical group that played guitars and a base and called themselves "The Potter's House Singers." The Potter's House was a coffee house in D.C.

Stan spent one year at William and Mary during which he applied to West Point. He was accepted as a qualified alternate. He graduated as a Second Lieutenant of Infantry qualifying as an Airborne, Ranger, and Special Forces officer. He retired from the Army after twenty-nine years as a Colonel of Special Forces being a "plank holder" in the Special Forces branch in 1988. He learned German while stationed in Germany.

I needed a car. My Dad went with me in September 1966, to Herby's Ford and he was silent while I made a "deal." I told the salesman that I wanted a '67 Mustang, I didn't have a down payment, I could afford $139 a month, which was taxi fare in Buffalo for a month, "Do you have a car for me?" He said yes: "three-by-the-knee, no air-conditioning, it has a radio and a heater." I said, "I'll take it." My Dad said, "Her mother and I would like to pay for white-wall tires." My brand new '67 Navy Blue Mustang with white-wall tires was gorgeous and I learned to drive a stick-shift.

In Washington I flew up and down the East Coast, often to Chicago and Detroit, and of course to New York's LaGuardia Airport. But sometimes I was invited to work "Special Assignments."

SPECIAL ASSIGNMENTS

These Special Assignments were on days off when work didn't involve flying. We had a very protective Base Manager, Clancy Henderson Melton who said, "Our stewardesses will not stand on a street corner, nor hand out literature, nor do housekeeping chores. But, they can wear their uniform and add social presence and congeniality to a business meeting." I didn't know it at the time, but the Gene Kelly screen test was a "special assignment."

Being selected to work an American Airlines reception for the Illinois Delegation was amazing. U.S. Senators, U.S. Representatives, and their staff flew on American so often that we became familiar with them flying to Chicago and back. The reception by American was a "Thank You" and many of our American Airlines company executives, both corporate and local (D.C.), came to the reception in the Capitol Building. We were a group of about six stewardesses and only we knew the hosts and guests. So, in uniform we took it upon ourselves to introduce American Airlines officers to the Senators and Congressmen.

Another Special Assignment: Lunch in the National Press Club! This was to introduce to the press American's new 747 service from Washington's Dulles Airport to Los Angeles. Walter Cronkite, Chet Huntley, and David Brinkley were there. I knew Chet Huntley's wife, Tippy Stringer, as she made a documentary film about our church in Alexandria, I had a short chat with Chet. We American Airlines stewardesses were there for presence in uniform and we were invited to have lunch as part of the honored guests.

Another Special Assignment: A company from California that sold avocados had a party in the afternoon and wanted American Airlines stewardesses in uniform to add class to their reception. Our new trip from D.C. to Los Angeles could create business for them and our job was to mingle. Well, we're not good at not doing anything so we started passing around trays of finger food and directing guests to the bar and introducing those we met to others.

We were not paid very much for our Special Assignments, but they were interesting and not a waste of time. American was proud to have us represent our company.

One of my trips while I was still living at home had a layover in Tulsa, Oklahoma. My Grandmother, a widow, lived on a farm by herself, in Terlton, Oklahoma, about an hour's driving time from the Tulsa airport, this is long before the new interstate highway was built. My

Auntie Agnes and Uncle Shell, who lived in Tulsa, met my flight and were with me as I rented a car, then they waved good bye. I drove out to visit and spend the night with my Grandmother. The roads were not paved in rural Oklahoma, and the ranches and farms were not close together.

Out on that unlit, dirt, one lane, lonesome road in November 1966 in a rented car, I ran out of gas.

In my uniform that looked like something from outer space with shiny blue high heels, big blue purse, electric blue suit with a white blouse and pearl buttons, and a pill box hat, I got out of the car and walked to the nearest farmhouse down the road. I didn't know this farm, I did know the people in the next farmhouse but that was another mile down the road. So, I walked down the lane to this house but there were dogs barking around the pickup trucks in the driveway and as I got closer the dogs started to jump up in front of me, all barking at the same time. That's why they have dogs, to scare off strangers wearing space suits.

No one came out to see what the problem was and I couldn't get close enough to knock on the door, so I started walking to the Ventres' farm down the road. Dirt roads with rocks in them are hard to walk on in high heels. Good news, a good ole boy came by, stopped and took me to the Ventres' farm, where they had a precious dog that seemed like he was waiting for company. Mr. Ventres didn't recognize me, but of course, knew my Grandmother and let me call her, but the best news is that he had some gas and took me back to my car and I was able to have a wonderful visit with my Grandmother.

I got back to the Tulsa airport with no trouble the next day, then home to my parent's house. When I walked in the door, my Dad called out, "How was the trip out to see Grandmother?" I said to Mother, "Come listen to this." My Dad came down the stairs two at a time with wide eyes, "What happened?" So I told them the story, my Dad almost turned inside out. He was the one raised out on that farm and could picture what I went through on that dirt road. What an experience!

Do you remember "Music 'Til Dawn?" American Airlines sponsored a radio program that began at Midnight and played until 6:00 in the morning. The theme song that was played as an introduction to the program was "That's All" by the Sy Mann Orchestra. I listened to "Music 'Til Dawn" when I was out late or on a date. The cities that broadcast it were: Boston, Washington, D.C., New York City, Chicago, Cincinnati, Detroit, Dallas, Los Angeles, and San Francisco from 1953 'til 1970.

In 1970, the Smithsonian Institute decided that they wanted to start a history of airline uniforms. The Air and Space Museum was being formulated by the Smithsonian to present the history of aviation in our country. Then, in 1971 the Smithsonian decided that they wanted the history of airline uniforms to be American Airlines.

When the Smithsonian contacted American at National Airport our supervisors didn't know if they could find the very first uniforms, but they did. One or two of our F/As' mothers were stewardesses long ago and had kept their uniforms. My supervisor knew that I had kept my uniforms and asked if I would donate my first uniform to the Smithsonian. They wanted the Navy-Blue winter uniform, I had graduated in the summer Light Blue uniform. I had kept them in case I had a little girl that might want to play dress-up in an old uniform or at least want to see it. Of course, I said yes, then she told me that they wanted everything: uniform with blouse, hat, coat, serving smock, scarf, with gloves, shoes, and underwear.

Underwear? When you think about it, the Smithsonian is authentic and back then, in 1965, we didn't have bikini panties, we had full panties, up to the waist, American Airlines Stewardesses were known for not being well endowed, so some of us had enhanced bras, we were required to wear a girdle with hook-up stockings, we were required to wear a full slip and all that is different today. I bought my first pair of pantyhose in Detroit three years later.

The Smithsonian asked for my name and address and a short paragraph about my career and where I had been based. My uniform is not on display as it is probably in a vault somewhere, but it is such an honor to have my uniform representing the American Airlines uniforms of 1965 in the Smithsonian Institute's Air and Space Museum.

Tina before trip to see Grandmother in Oklahoma

Family 1967

Mimi, Hayward, Tina and Stan

In front of National Airport, 1968

Passenger took this picture in 1968 and sent it to me addressed to
American Airlines National Airport

The Vatican has granted special dispensation to Roman Catholics on American Airlines from the obligation of abstinence on all Fridays and other days of abstinence. On future flights, should you prefer seafood, please make this known at the time of making your reservation. We will be glad to accommodate you.

Vatican
dispensation for
Roman Catholic
passengers

Vatican note on every tray about not eating meat on Fridays

Uniform in the Smithsonian

Uniform in the Smithsonian

Uniform in the Smithsonian

Easy Victor

During our extensive, incredible training for the 747, I took a management test and qualified to become a "1st Flight Attendant." Of course, there is a First Flight Attendant on every plane who fills out reports and forms, turns in the money, makes announcements, and reports to the Captain. But the 747 was different: more passengers, more F/As, and the need to have someone "in charge" (as in: "I want to speak to whoever is in charge!") In the beginning we were called, "First Lady" then this position was called "The Premium" because we received extra or premium pay, then it settled down to "1st Flight Attendant." And then…on International Flights we were/are called "Purser." Along with extra pay and responsibilities we received extra training and had extra meetings.

Our Washington, D.C. base was one of American's first to be awarded a Boeing 747 trip and it was out of Dulles (IAD) airport to Los Angeles (LAX), flown by LAX cockpit crew and DCA (Washington) Flight Attendants.

Training on the Boeing-747 was amazing, everything was different, we had 14 Flight Attendants, we had 366 seats, a downstairs galley, in fact two of them, one for First Class and one for Coach. Each galley on the lower level had two elevators, one for personnel and one for carts. The personnel elevator was just that, for us to go up and down to the galley. The cart elevators were a little taller than the height of a cart and were not completely closed in as the personnel elevators were. The elevators were controlled by push-buttons located in the "service center" and down in the galley, and inside the personnel elevator. Now that I have said that, the elevators presented a learning situation for we Flight Attendants and maintenance. The elevators broke, often, and we didn't have time for that! We mostly had trouble with the "cart elevators." But we had hundreds of people to serve and didn't have time to figure out the problems. When we wrote in the maintenance log that the elevators were broken, maintenance guys were looking out at the tail at "the elevators" also known as the horizontal stabilizers. So the first thing we had to do was re-name our elevators to: "lifts." It sounds like this was accomplished in one or two trips, no, this took a couple of months.

Much of the work of preparing the carts for the service was done in the galley; beverage carts were sent up to start the service right after take- off while the entrees were being heated up and the bread warmed and the coffee made for the meal service which would start maybe an hour after the beverage service. For the meal service, tray carts had to be "pre-positioned" in the front of the coach section, on both sides of the airplane, then two in the middle (near the service center), then two more in the aft (back) of the plane, near the "lounge." Yes, we had a lounge behind the last row of seats in coach.

The lounge was surprisingly big and about a year after the 747 was introduced a piano was added to the lounge. For the inaugural of the piano, on our Flight 75 to Los Angeles, American Airlines hired Frank Sinatra, Jr. to play and sing on the airplane. WOW! We didn't have famous personalities on our flights to perform after that, but the passengers could play the piano if they wanted to and many did, some good and some not so good, mostly very entertaining.

History: American had always wanted to serve hot rolls on the meal trays but there was never enough room in the ovens to heat the entrees and rolls to be ready and the right temperature at the same time. After all these years, finally, there was a way on the 747 with all the ovens and pre-heated carts and foil bags to heat the rolls and put them in the carts. We had so many passengers the foil bags of warm bread didn't fit in the entree carts; another cart had to be added to the parade of carts to serve lunch or dinner. Another problem was to fit all our beverages in and on top of the beverage cart, with soft drinks, orange juice, water, liquor, beer, wine, and coffee. We added the wine to the bread cart and called it the "Communion" Cart.

So here is the parade: the tray cart, entree cart, Communion cart, and beverage cart. It was a sight to see. This parade was on both sides of the airplane in Coach. There were usually three entree choices, steak, chicken, and fish. We had to really work as a team to have all the choices available until they ran out and to have the tray carts ready to switch out. Sometimes the Flight Attendants in First Class would come back and start coffee seconds and even pick up trays if they had time.

Compared to Coach, First Class was not as complicated. The beverage service for years was served by hand running the beverage on a tray, not using a cart, then we started using a cart in each aisle and the service went much faster.

First Class Flight Attendants provided hot towels to every passenger, set each tray table by hand starting with a table cloth, knives and forks, and wine glass, then tossed the salad in the aisle from a three-tiered cart. The three-tiered cart was used again for the entree service while cutting the roast beef at the passenger's seat. These details, along with caviar as an appetizer or smoked salmon with caviar on top, do make a difference and sets the First Class section apart. Our signature dessert was always an Ice Cream Sundae, maybe with a choice of toppings prepared and served in the aisle.

First Class also had a lounge, it was up the winding staircase, next to the cockpit, with couches and a place to set up a serve-yourself bar. Many took advantage of the lounge and enjoyed the unique atmosphere in flight while visiting with other passengers. Years later, the couches were taken out and seats were added.

There was an element on the 747 that we were not used to: the interior of the cabin had a slight angle or incline, it was hardly noticeable at first, then we started talking about the angle. It was hard to explain, like walking up hill. Until, we had proof!

The cockpit crews that flew these trips on the 747 were based in Los Angeles, we flew with the same crew often and they were very senior in Los Angeles. These senior pilots had their pick of trips and schedules. One month we flew with the same crew a couple of times and found out that the Captain was going to retire after our next trip. We Flight Attendants planned a little "Surprise Party" for him at the end of his last trip. Different Flight Attendants brought decorations, a bottle of bourbon, some cards we all signed, and I bought a cake mix that all you had to do was add water, the box even included the little aluminum pan, with all of the directions. I bought icing to spread on the top and alphabet letters made of sugar. The whole purpose of this was to bake the cake on the airplane, not just buy one and bring it to the party. We told the co-pilot and the flight-engineer our plans, right after the passengers were off to not leave the airplane before the party.

I did make a P.A. to the passengers that it was the Captain's last flight, the passengers clapped and we told him about it when he came down the staircase, a few passengers had waited to shake his hand. We quickly set up our little party, with some soft drinks, and napkins. Well, the Captain was overwhelmed! On the cake the little letters said, "Good Luck John." But the corker was that the cake baked at an angle! Who would have guessed! Anyway, the Captain didn't want to eat it, he wanted to take it with him for his official retirement party with his friends and family and to show off his cake that was baked on board his last flight and it was at an angle to prove it.

Another detail about this new 747 was the movie delivery system.

The movie film actually moved through the airplane. Down one side across the back and up the other side. How this worked I still can't figure out, but we had little or no problem with the presentation of the movies on board. The screens were located above about every fifth row in coach. The screens in First Class were bigger, we didn't need as many. There were no movie screens in the upstairs lounge nor in the coach lounge. We had to sell headsets in coach after boarding and before take-off.

These long non-stops, including the coast to coast trips out of New York's Kennedy Airport, and Boston to Los Angeles and San Francisco on our new 747s had so many passengers that American started a new program of having a person on board who could talk to passengers about ticketing and reservations. This person was not part of the crew, in fact we could leave without this person if he or she didn't show up for some reason. This position was called the "Flight Service Director."

Our Flight 75 on August 21, 1973 Washington to Los Angeles was full as usual and proceeded as normal, I was 1st Flight Attendant. Our landing was normal, or so we thought. As I was making the "taxi-in P.A." the Captain broke in to my P.A. saying, "Flight Service Director come to the cockpit immediately!" There was stress in his voice. If there is a problem, he is supposed to call me, 1st Flight Attendant or even another Flight Attendant, but not the Flight Service Director, he (or she) hadn't been trained in Emergency Procedures and took no training with us. But, there was no time to debate this. The Flight Service Director ran up the stairs to the cockpit, and I told the 1st Class Flight Attendants to go to their exits and to tell the other Flight Attendants that they saw on the way to their exits to go to their exits. I didn't make a P.A. because I didn't know if we were going to have to evacuate or not, or what was the matter. I turned around to check my exit, and where we were on the ground: Runway? Taxi-way? As I checked, the Flight Service Director was coming down the circular stairway three steps at a time and said, "We have a fire in the cargo compartment and we have to evac..."

The Captain made a P.A. "Easy Victor! Easy Victor!" This was our signal from the Cockpit to evacuate. I turned around, facing my huge door that was all prepared to open and the slide to deploy, I put both hands on the handle, and rotated the handle, the automatic door opener kicked in and the door opened with me still holding it! As I started going out with the door, I quickly let go and watched this magnificent slide unfold from its cover in the door, burst into action, and touch the ground at the perfect angle. Our passengers in First Class were ready to go as soon as the slide stopped moving, but they all had their purses, briefcases, etc. with them. Our training teaches us that they can't take anything with them, as it could hurt them in the evacuation, or rip the slide, so I started yelling, as were the other Flight Attendants: "Unfasten Seat Belts, Come This Way, Remove shoes, Don't Take Anything With You!" To the first ones in line to evacuate we added: "You, You, stay at the bottom, help the people off the slide!"

By the end and all people off, the area was littered with their carry-on items.

Before I evacuated, I ran through my First Class cabin to make sure everyone was out, and, as you can imagine, Coach was still evacuating. I saw down the right aisle a mother carrying a big carry-on bag and dragging her son, who was blind, to the exit. The child, maybe 10 or 11 years old, didn't understand what was happening and was grabbing and clinging to seat-backs, slowing their progress to the closest exit. As others were flinging themselves into the slide at Door 2-R, I ran back to the row where they were stopped, took the carry-on from her and they quickly got to the exit. The blind youngster couldn't see the open door or slide and had to be coaxed/pushed without going head-first, so we had him sit down on the exit, and the Flight Attendant pushed him over the edge. Although he did start going sideways, he made it down safely.

We were on the taxi-way and a TWA 747 landed right after us. The tower hadn't closed the runway yet, so the TWA airplane had to turn around at the end of the runway. Some of our passengers were so frightened that they just kept running and were under the wing of the turning TWA airplane.

Once the Flight Attendants had evacuated, we were able to corral our passengers and check to see if there were any injuries. As I was checking my passengers, one man grabbed me and said, "You have got to get me a drink!" This sounds like a joke and my first thought was to laugh, but this guy was serious. Oh, what a problem he had. I said, "You have to hold yourself together until you get into the terminal, you know I can't help you out here."

The only passenger injury was a broken ankle, a lady stood up from the slide at 2-L wrong and her ankle snapped. Several passengers had trouble standing up at that slide, and the Flight Attendant manning that slide dislocated her thumb getting up out of the slide.

There was no fire. The Captain told us once we were in the airport, in Operations, that about the time we started our descent into Los Angeles, a fire alarm, with lights and bells, started in the cockpit indicating that there was a fire in the aft cargo compartment. While the Captain continued the descent and approach to the runway, the First Officer and Flight Engineer "fought the fire" from the cockpit, with the equipment and procedures for fighting the fire with Halon chemical fire-extinguishers positioned in the cargo-compartment. The Captain told the tower we were probably going to have to evacuate when the aircraft cleared the runway because he couldn't be certain that there was a fire or that it was out. And, he didn't want to take the airplane to the gate not knowing what was happening in the cargo compartment. A smart decision.

Later, with no one else around, I asked the Captain why he called for the Flight Service Director, who was based in Los Angeles, to go to the cockpit and not me, he said, "I know him, I don't know you."

It all worked out for the best, as most of the Flight Attendants were at their doors when we got the call: "Easy Victor!"

The Vietnam Chapter

The Vietnam Chapter

The timing of our involvement in Vietnam is fuzzy as I don't remember a "starting gun." It was like "trickle boarding," we didn't start all at the same time, we trickled in until we were "all on-board," so to speak.

By the time I transferred to Washington, D.C. there were military guys on board our flights in uniform leaving home, going to their bases or departure points throughout the United States. In some cases, it was the first time they had been on an airplane. Many came to D.C. on their way to Andrews Air Force Base, some to Philadelphia on their way to Fort Monmouth, New Jersey, or Fort Dix.

Although I flew often to Chicago or New York, I preferred a trip that eventually spent the night in Memphis, Tennessee at the Peabody Hotel. The Peabody meant so much to me as my parents had their honeymoon there, my grandparents had their 50th wedding anniversary there, and on occasion when my family visited my grandparents in Memphis, we ate dinner on the roof at the Peabody. Then it was always fun to see the Ducks parade out of the elevator to march around the lobby fountain.

The trip started in Washington, then flew to Philadelphia, so here we go, this is all in one day:

Washington, D.C. (DCA)
Philadelphia, Penn. (PHL) Ate lunch (Philly steak and cheese)
Washington, D.C. (DCA)
Charleston, W. Va. (CRW) In winter it got dark on approach
Knoxville, Tenn. (TYS)
Nashville, Tenn. (BNA) Pilots brought us ice cream sandwiches
Memphis, Tenn. (MEM) Keep going!
Little Rock, Ark. (LIT) In summer it got dark while here
Memphis, Tenn. (MEM)

This was an old Southern Mail Route, the mail went on to Dallas, then to the west coast. The next day we retraced our flight (MEM-LIT-MEM-BNA-TYS-CRW-DCA) and got off in Washington, a new crew took over up to PHL and on with the above stops.

It was late when we arrived downtown at the Peabody, but we changed our clothes and went into the alley behind the hotel to the Rendezvous for ribs! We did this every trip as this place has been famous for their Barbeque since 1948.

During the years I flew this trip, Vietnam was requiring more and more of our young men and women. Sometimes we Flight Attendants flew together long enough to become good friends. One friend, Janet Rogala, was going with a Marine. Her Marine left for Vietnam and they often corresponded with tapes (no cell phones, computers, or videos). Then, one month that Janet and I flew together (four trips) she brought her tape from her Marine officer and we listened to it, he had several other Marines with him on the tape, so the three stewardesses on our trip in Memphis made up a "party" in our room at the Peabody to laugh and tell stories. We listened to their tape, made a new tape, and Janet sent it to her Marine in Vietnam.

As month after month proceeded, a military guy (a few girls, not many) boarded our airplane on every trip, sometimes more than one.

Sometimes they sat together, sometimes they only gave a small, knowing, acknowledgement with a nod, or touch his forehead, or hat (cover).

On one occasion, in Memphis, during boarding, a soldier boarded and took his seat in coach, then the gate agent came running on board to get the soldier. His mother had fainted and was out cold back in the gate area. She rallied when he got there, she sat up and talked with her son for a few minutes. He re-boarded, then we heard her screaming from the gate. Our soldier went back out to the gate to console her, all the while we were boarding other passengers. Then the agent told the soldier and his family that he had to make a decision. He came down the jet bridge with the agent to close the door. Oh, the heartache that soldier must have felt.

Memphis again:

This was an incredible sight! Twins — soldiers — in uniform boarded. They were all smiles, they made little jokes. On the way to their seats other passengers patted them on the back, smiling, made comments, and a few clapped. Each brother was so proud of the other.

Charleston, West Virginia:

This soldier boarded in Philadelphia on his way home from Vietnam to Little Rock, Arkansas. Our airplane was a BAC-111, a smaller jet with the twin-engines on the tail, it had its own integral stairs that deployed when you opened the front door. Charleston didn't have jet bridges, but, we didn't need them anyway. The Charleston bound passengers got off, then the agent came up the stairs and announced that the outbound flight was going to be full and all military and stand-by (reduced rate) passengers had to get off. Our soldier dutifully got off. We were so sad — many passengers patted him on the back, the pilots shook his hand. Then we boarded our out bound passengers that were going to our stops on the way to Little Rock. The agent came up the stairs with the PRR (passenger revenue report) paperwork, then back down the stairs to close the door. Someone yelled out "We have an empty seat!!" I yelled down to the agent, "Wait! we have an empty seat! Go get the soldier!" The agent said, it's too late we have to close it up! I said — yelled — "You go get him, we'll wait!" The agent went off to find him, then came back and said that he couldn't find him. I yelled down the stairs — "We are going to wait until he is on this airplane, look in the bathroom, on the phone, in the bar — you find him, his Mama's waiting for him in Little Rock!" I yelled all this then I asked the pilots if it's O.K.? They said, "We'll wait!" Well, the agent found him in the restroom, and that soldier came running! When he got to the top of the stairs the passengers went wild!

I flew this flight long enough that I actually brought some of the same guys back home. Some observations: When they came back they were pale, a strange paleness. I asked my doctor about this and how consistent this was and he said it is called the "Pallor of War." Another worrisome detail is that many of our soldiers threw-up on the way home. Most slept. On occasion a passenger would send him a beer.

The twins. I had the honor of working the trip that brought the twins home. However, one twin was the official escort of the body of his brother. Our twin in the cabin was stoic as he got off the airplane to perform his difficult duty. The protocol was for the escort to be the first passenger off the airplane, he was to proceed down the outside stairs of the jet bridge, and on to the cargo door where the casket was removed with escort waiting. The passengers on this airplane didn't get off immediately as they watched out of the right-side windows for the brother's casket to emerge from the airplane. Flag draped. There wasn't a dry eye, this was heart wrenching. It's hard to go on after telling about the twins...

On another occasion, I remember an escort on board into Oklahoma City. The passengers didn't know this soldier was on duty; they all deplaned as normal. When they were all off, I sat down at the window to see the escort soldier riding "shot-gun" (the right side front seat, an old American term from the stage-coach days) with the cargo guy driving the Flag draped coffin away from the airplane. That picture, along with the twins, has stayed with me.

I agonized constantly over taking these guys away from home.

I wanted to work the trips going over to Vietnam. They were charter trips as the government contracted with American Airlines to take troops and equipment by the airplane load. The contract was called MAC (Military Airlift Command). I wasn't senior enough. Stewardesses who had been Supervisors for years went back "on the line" in order to qualify to work trips to Vietnam. That honor remained very senior.

As Vietnam progressed, we were hearing of soldiers and pilots "missing in action." Then "POWs," prisoners of war, Air Force pilots, Soldiers, Navy pilots, and Marines were being described in the news. Picturing their circumstances kept me up at night, as it did many Americans.

In honor of our POWs we started wearing copper bracelets with a POWs name on it and the date he went missing. My POW's name was Charles Hoskins from Shawnee Mission, Kansas, missing as of: 2-16-71.

I didn't find out about what happened to him until the traveling Vietnam Wall of Honor came to Bonita Springs, Florida, near Naples where I now live. He didn't come home.

American Airlines even added a "detention briefing" to our yearly emergency procedures training. It was not likely that Stewardesses would be tortured, as we wouldn't know any military information, but we could be detained for a length of time. I remember some of the things our training suggested that we occupy our time or thoughts with:

1. Plan a wedding in detail.
2. In your mind: build something or write a book.

3. Analyze the coloring of your surroundings.
4. Enjoy any kind of contact with other detainees.
5. Make cards or game pieces out of anything you can find.
6. In your mind find "a place to go" that lifts your spirits.
7. If you are religious, rely on your faith for coping skills.

I am sure they gave us more information to train us, these are the things I recall. I have used some of these when I couldn't sleep or when waiting in a doctors' office.

Worrying about POW's became a daily subject of conversation among many of my stewardess friends. We had military guys on most trips. Back then, nothing to do with the military, American and other carriers had small boxes of cigarettes on each lunch and dinner tray. These small boxes made by different cigarette companies had three cigarettes in them. Some passengers didn't take the cigarette boxes from their tray, so at the end of every service, when we picked up the trays, we collected the small boxes that were left and gave them to the military guys on board.

Smoking was allowed on board then, the cabins were not divided into "smoking and non-smoking," people even smoked in the lavatory!

Flying, while based in Washington, D.C., provided many humbling opportunities to admire the courage of the United States Military.

Twice I worked trips that brought a young man and his entire family to D.C. to be awarded the Medal of Honor by President Nixon. In both cases, the soldier sat with his eyes closed as if asleep while the family was wide eyed with excitement. One of these families had never flown before.

My parents were living in Honolulu, Hawaii from 1972 -1974. Of course, I visited them often and on every visit we talked about Vietnam and about the POWs. When the war was officially over and the day had finally come to bring the POWs home, I watched every minute of the television coverage. In fact, my mother and I were watching it "together" on TV, she in Hawaii, on the phone, and me in my apartment in Alexandria, Virginia. At one point, she said: "Hold on, here comes the plane!" She was seeing the actual airplane in Hawaii flying parallel to Waikiki Beach while I was watching it on my television.

I am going to fast forward here to tell about a former POW, who is now a neighbor of mine in Sterling Oaks, a gated tennis community in Naples, Florida.

Luis Chirichigno was born in Peru but went to college at the University of Alabama and played football there under Paul "Bear" Bryant. We call him "Jerry," and his wife, Maria, both play tennis in Sterling Oaks and when Jerry is playing on one of our 12 courts, it's like we are all at attention to honor him. Jerry lost a finger with other injuries in his helicopter that was shot down. He was captured and put in a Vietnam POW cage. His incredible story is documented "on line" and in the Military Heritage Museum in Punta Gorda, Florida. Jerry donated his pink and gray striped POW uniform and his "HO CHI MINH" sandals, made from tires, to the museum. To accompany Jerry's personal donations, a cabinet maker from Port Charlotte, Florida made a bamboo cage to replicate Jerry's 3' by 4' by 5' cage. The bamboo was ordered from Vietnam.

I drove up to Punta Gorda to visit the Military Heritage Museum and to see the presentation about Jerry. I was directed to the back of the Museum and as I approached the "cage" I burst into tears.

Until you stand in front of the cage that our POWs endured you can't conceive of their inner strength and the strength of our Military.

Oh, there are lots of 747 stories that I'll share later, but none as important or as meaningful as this:

Our crew, our 747, had the breathtaking honor of taking our POWs who lived on the west coast to Washington, D.C. to meet President Nixon! As you can imagine, the President wanted to see them right away, so they hadn't been home very long, ten days? Two weeks? Most were accompanied by their wives. One man's parents were with him. First Class was made exclusively for them and we didn't make any announcements about them being on board. Details:

They came up the jet bridge quiet and subdued with big eyes in wonder holding their wife's hand. The Captain stood with me at the front door to greet them. Most of these guys were pilots so seeing our beautiful spiral staircase up to the lounge and cockpit was amazing.

I don't know if the wives were briefed but with almost every couple, she didn't take her hand away from his, always touching, constant contact.

Leaving LAX was a lunch flight, we left Los Angeles about 9:30 am but that was already 12:30 in D.C. so, we proceeded with our beverage service, then lunch. Remaining subdued, we found out they hadn't seen or talked to each other since they returned home. After lunch things changed. They got up and moved around, shook hands, hugged, went upstairs to the lounge. The lounge was small, at that time there were only two couches facing each other and a rounded couch across the back. The Captain let them see the cockpit...pilots, you know. Wives visited with each other but they were not out of sight of their guy...except one couple...strange, right after take-off, she went upstairs, in a few minutes, he went upstairs, she came down. She didn't eat, he did. As time went on, she sat and read, he visited with the guys.

The trip became like a cocktail party with very little drinking. They did smoke, but mostly talked and started laughing and holding on to their wife and their new life and freedom.

What an Honor.

Before I close this "Chapter," I want to mention a couple of my friends.

Remember the trip to Memphis? The trip had been upgraded to a Boeing 727 and, probably in the fall of 1966, a tall, handsome, Naval

Academy Midshipman in uniform, boarded in Memphis. We already had something in common, Memphis. I think there was another Midshipman with him, they were on their way back to Annapolis. We had a nice visit as I worked through Nashville, Knoxville, Charleston, and then D.C. The Midshipmen got off in D.C. When I got off the airplane "Alan" was at the bottom of the stairs (no jet bridges yet). He asked me if he could see me again. When I said yes, we made plans.

Alan taught me to sail some small boats, I met his family in Memphis, he was on the football team. It was amazing to go to his football games, especially the Army-Navy Game! I was honored to be his date for his graduation.

He went Navy Air out of the Academy and recently I asked him (via e-mail) about his time during Vietnam. This is what he said, "I joined my first P-3 squadron on deployment in Naha Okinawa. My squadron, VP-22 (the Blue Geese) was based in Barbers Point, Hawaii. On that deployment, we patrolled mostly in the South China Sea off Vietnam. We flew designated tracks, identifying all shipping along the track. Occasionally we patrolled off the coast of Russia." He was deployed three times.

After the Navy, Alan flew with United Airlines. Through many challenges in both of our lives we have stayed in touch and are friends to this day. Something constant in all these years is that we bet on the Army—Navy Game.

GO ARMY!

Remember that my Brother, Stan, graduated from West Point. Although they trained all four years preparing to go to war, his class was the first class to not go to Vietnam since the war started. Stan's daughter graduated from West Point and married a West Point grad. Did I say: "GO ARMY?!"

Sigh...There was a guy in high school that I had a crush on, like most guys that girls have a crush on in high school, he didn't know I was alive. He was on the football team and maybe knew I was a neighbor. After high school he went to VMI (Virginia Military Institute), graduated in 1965, and qualified to fly for the Air Force just as Vietnam was ramping up.

"Billy" became a C-123 pilot and was awarded the Silver Star for saving some of our trapped Marines who were pinned down, attacked and injured. Billy went against orders. Here is the way he put it in a letter he wrote to me dated June 19, 1968 (I saved all his letters):

"Last week I almost 'cashed in.' We landed and we were mortared at the same time. I suppose some of the rounds were rockets. Anyhow, we found ourselves stuck out on the runway (dirt strip) like a perfect target. I haven't figured out how they kept missing though they didn't miss by much. Here's hoping my luck and time in Vietnam run out together."

Billy's good friend and lawyer, and also a good friend of mine in Alexandria, Karl Weickhardt, sent me more information in a letter about this incredible day: "Billy received an urgent request from a Marine company to pick up ammunition it had stashed in the jungle. Billy found the ammunition and flew it to the requested location. When he arrived over the scene the Marines were surrounded and taking heavy fire, including the mortar fire. Billy told the Marine company commander that his regulations prohibited him from landing in the middle of a firefight. The C-123 was a huge target. The Marine captain replied, 'I don't know about your regulations, Lieutenant, but if we don't get that ammunition we'll all be dead by nightfall.' Billy then announced that he was going to land and asked for covering fire. While they were unloading, a mortar round exploded next to the plane. One of Billy's crew members jumped out of the plane into the mortar crater. His burly crew chief jumped out after the airman, picked him up and threw him back in the plane and they took off. Although the plane sustained some damage from the small arms fire, neither Billy nor any member of his crew was wounded." He was awarded the Silver Star and the Distinguished Flying Cross.

After Vietnam we dated, but just as the song, "By the time I get to Phoenix" became popular, Billy was transferred to Luke Air Force Base near Phoenix. He lived out the song (but going West) by skipping our last date. Sometime later, in a letter, he said, "I should have taken you to Phoenix with me."

Billy went on to fly for Southern Airways and the several airlines that eventually became Northwest Airlines. He loved to talk to my Dad about flying in WWII, Billy called my Dad, "Wiley" as in Wiley Post the old aviator from Oklahoma.

Billy died April 6, 2006 and is buried in Arlington National Cemetery.

He never married.

"The Vietnam Chapter" is dedicated to our military, with their strength they hold us together and keep us strong.

In 747 Upper Lounge
Tina, Leslie Lowman, Lois Hollister, Janet Rogala

EPTs on Board

Our Emergency Procedure Training (EPT) included classroom training as well as hands-on training on the actual airplane. This was before American set up simulators at our training academy in Ft. Worth.

For years we assembled in a hangar at our bases late at night to await the airplanes arriving from their day's work and we could climb on board to handle each piece of emergency equipment. We had to locate the oxygen bottles, which are in different locations on different types of aircraft. We had to locate and operate water and chemical fire extinguishers.

We also had to arm and disarm the doors, this means "attach the slide." Then we had to practice opening the doors as different airplane types have different ways to open the door, even the handles are different. On some we rotate a handle and the door opens outward, on others we pull a handle and the door slides up into the fuselage. After we activate the handle, most doors open automatically and the slide also deploys automatically.

During this practice (EPT) on the airplane there were occasions when something we used broke, then maintenance would come on the airplane and fix it. This could cause a delay for the next outbound trip.

I worked one of the trips that changed having EPT on the airplane.

This flight was my old favorite, Flight 75 from Washington's Dulles Airport (IAD) to LAX. It was a new DC-10 with a full load.

Our crew boarded the airplane just as a Washington based EPT class was finishing their hands-on training. Their EPT was in the afternoon after the airplane came in from LAX. Of course their training included arming and disarming the door, they used door 2L, the second door on the left side.

Almost immediately after the training class left the airplane, the passengers arrived on the Mobile Lounge. This is a bus-like conveyance to move the passengers to and from the airport concourse to the gates which are located remotely from the airport building.

Soon we were ready to go. I was 1st F/A and our procedures were to wait until the airplane was moving forward before we armed the doors. We started moving so I made the "Prepare for departure" P.A.

Note: Now the "Prepare for departure" P.A. is made when the boarding door is closed and the agent pulls the jet bridge away, but the Pilot hasn't released the brakes.

As soon as I said "Prepare for Departure," the F/A at door 2L armed her door, and the emergency signaling system went off. She yelled, "It's my door!" I was still in the First Class aisle going to my door at 1L to arm it. The emergency signaling system was screaming! The airplane stopped with a jolt, then the Flight Engineer bolted out of the cockpit and yelled across First Class, "Who turned on the signaling system? What's the emergency?"

Our procedures are that with the emergency signaling system on, if the airplane stops, we open the doors and proceed with the evacuation and if one door opens then all doors must open and start the evacuation.

We in the front of the airplane knew that Carol's door was the problem, and there was no problem in the cockpit, but the over-wing F/As and the back of the airplane didn't know there was no "real" problem. The F/As working in coach at doors 4L and 4R opened their doors and started the evacuation procedures: "Unfasten seatbelts, come this way, don't bring anything with you, remove shoes!" One man blew right by the F/A at door 4L with his briefcase handcuffed to his arm and jumped into the slide. (This was Washington, D.C., maybe he had top secret information in his briefcase.)

I remembered the evacuation in Los Angles on the 747 when the cockpit thought we had a fire in the cargo compartment and I know that people can get hurt in an evacuation. There was no need for this evacuation.

I made a P.A. to stop evacuating: "Do not evacuate! Do not evacuate!" The passengers in the middle of the airplane could hear both commands: in the back, "Come this way!" in the front, "Do not evacuate!" They didn't know what to do. The F/As with over-wing responsibilities told their passengers to stay in their seats.

All these F/As were my friends and we had worked together for years. Lois in the back got on the P.A. and said, "Are we supposed to evacuate or not?" I also made a P.A and said, "No, Lois, there is no emergency, stop the evacuation."

We had 30 people on the ground, none hurt, but we also had two slides deployed and three engines running. The Captain shut down the engines and ground personnel took care of our passengers. The Mobile Lounges came out to get the passengers on the airplane. In the terminal, they waited for another airplane to take them to Los Angeles.

The slides had to be repacked, which would take hours and the emergency signaling system had to be reset. The arming mechanism had to be fixed, and the airplane may have had to go to Tulsa for American Airlines maintenance to do the work or check that it was exactly right.

Our cockpit crew and F/As assembled in American's Operations.

Now we had to write reports. My report was hard to write as no matter how I worded it, it looked like the fault was that the Captain stopped the airplane. The problem really was that "door 2L's" arming mechanism broke during EPTs and the next time it was "armed" the signaling system went off.

I got in trouble for stopping the evacuation. Supervisors even sent me back to Ft. Worth to retake EPTs. This was to re-calibrate my brain that "if one evacuates, we all evacuate." Okay, I got it.

After the EPT training. The Supervisors came to me and said that I had done the right thing for those circumstances and that nothing negative was going to be in my file, not even the additional training.

Now we have simulators to practice on in Ft. Worth, no more EPTs on board the airplane.

One Enchanted Morning

After flying back and forth to Los Angeles all month, I flew to see my parents in Hawaii at the end of July 1974 on some days off. I took my trusty Flight 75 out of Dulles to LAX and spent the night at our layover hotel, The Airport Marina Hotel near the airport. On the airplane to LAX in First Class was a friend of mine that was going to see her husband who was in the military in Korea. We had a nice chat and decided to share the cost of the hotel room near the airport as she also had an early trip in the morning.

On July 27, 1974, we arrived at our gates extra early to sign-in for our separate trips in order to improve our chances for stand-by seats. Now, we had about two hours to wait.

Let's go to the coffee shop! The coffee shop was packed. We looked and looked for a place to sit, and way in the back, across the crowded room, was a table with one gorgeous man sitting there. I made my way to his side, as strange as it seems, and said (famous first-words), "Are you expecting anyone?"

He said no, so Heather sat down with all our "stuff," carry-on, sweaters, purses. I did take money to buy coffee, sweet rolls, orange juice, etc. When I finally sat down, this man said, "So where do you fly?" I said, "I've been flying to L.A. twice a week for four years... you have an accent, where are you from?" He said, "I'm from Ireland, but I live in L.A."

During a short chat, we learned that he was going to see his parents who were visiting his sister in Toronto, they were from Belfast, Northern Ireland. He also had business in Toronto the next week.

I asked him how he liked living in LA? He said it was okay, but he wouldn't want to raise a family there, it's too crowded. (Does that mean he's single?)

We found out he was an electronic engineer in sales, he worked for N.V. Philips and sold test equipment to the aerospace industry. In some ways, it was like there were only the two of us in that coffee shop.

All of a sudden he said, "I've got to go, he looked at me and said, "Can I call you when you are in LA?" Well, I'm a Virginia lady, I can't be picked up in a coffee shop in 40 minutes! I remember thinking: if I say no, that's it, I won't see him again, I won't find out any more about him, I won't be able to look into his blue eyes. (I've started some tears as I write this).

O.K., keep going...

I said, yes. He asked when will I be back in L.A.? He said, how can he call me and his name is Bill McNeice. I gave him my formal calling card:

Miss Amelia Justina Florer

Nothing else was on the card, so I put my home number in Virginia on the card and said that I might be back on August 4th, I didn't know my schedule for August yet.

Yes, our first date was August 4, 1974. I was 28, and I had been flying for almost nine years.

Bill had trouble finding my hotel. When he called that he was in the lobby, most of my crew came to the lobby to meet him!

The two of us went out for a drink, it was about 9:30 and when he found out I hadn't eaten, we ordered hamburgers. I saw Bill every evening I was in L.A., which was twice a week, then I had weekends off in D.C.

I say evening, as these were late dinner dates, all over the airport area, mostly at the Marina by the boats. He had rented sailboats on his days off while living in L.A. and he enjoyed telling me about his adventures sailing off the coast of L.A. We walked around the Marina some nights.

He was a perfect gentleman, divorced, had two boys who lived in Pennsylvania. He lived in "the Valley" (San Fernando Valley) which was pretty far from the airport. We Flight Attendants still shared a room on our lay-overs, so our time together was over dinner.

His birthday was in July, mine was August 19th. He knew my birthday was August 19 but I was in L.A. on the 18th, so we raised our glass to my birthday on the 18th. He was nervous as he pulled a present out of his pocket. It was a platinum and diamond cross with a sterling silver necklace chain! It was the most beautiful, thoughtful surprise I ever had. He knew I was Christian. We had talked about it many times, but he wasn't, and when I asked him about this beautiful cross, he said the cross was a symbol of love and he wanted me to have it from him.

It was an Enchanted Evening

The very next weekend my parents left Hawaii and started their move back to the east coast as my Dad had retired in June from the FAA. We had planned it so that they would be passengers on my flight 76 from L.A. to D.C. In all the years that I had been flying, my Dad had never used one of my passes, this was going to be the first time. When Bill found out they were going to spend the night in L.A., he asked what was my Dad's favorite liquor, I said whiskey and Bill bought my Dad a bottle of Scotch. My Dad was thrilled! None of my other boyfriends had thought of him before, and not only that, Bill brought my mother flowers. What a guy!!

This introduction was made in my parents' hotel room, the Sheraton Americana, at the airport, it was late so we didn't have a lot of time together that night, but I did take my mother into their bathroom to show her the cross. I told her, "I have brought home a lot of guys for them to meet, and I'm not saying, 'This is it.' But, pay attention, look at him, hear his voice, listen to his Irish accent, look at the way he looks at me. So you won't say, 'which one is he?'" We laughed but she said she already liked him … how old is he? 37, and now I'm 29 …

I was able to pre-board my parents before our Flight 76 back to D.C., the flowers came with us and the bottle of Scotch was easily packed. Oh, how times have changed!

The crew all wanted to meet my parents, and the cockpit crew especially wanted to meet my Dad. It was fun having them on my flight. My mother had been my traveling companion for all these years, and with my Dad on board, I knew it was a Check Ride. Now they were on their way to Ft. Myers, Florida where they would start their newly retired lifestyle.

Why Ft. Myers? That's a good story: After my brother graduated from West Point, my Dad, Hayward Florer, accepted a post in Hawaii with the FAA's headquarters for the Pacific Region. His new job was, FAA Chief of the Pacific for Flight Standards. While he was in this position Vietnam was slowing down but our POWs had not been released so he was focused on that area.

Before he retired, Hayward visited all his offices in the Pacific region and during his meeting with his man in Tokyo, the man asked Hayward where he was going to retire? "Somewhere in Florida," Hayward said, "we loved Florida when we were based there during WWII and we promised ourselves we would move back some day, but I don't know where in Florida, we'll start in Miami." This man in Tokyo said,

"I just bought a condo in Ft. Myers and my wife and I won't retire for two years, would you like to move into our new condo until you find a permanent place?" So, they rented his new condo and loved Ft. Myers.

Every trip to see Bill in L.A. was so exciting I was falling in love with him, but, still, strictly dinner and maybe a walk, with lots of talking. Then, during the dinner on September 14, he asked me to marry him, he couldn't stand the distance and this timing any longer! I said, "Can I tell you next week?" His face fell, but said "Okay, is there something wrong?"

What he didn't know was that I had the honor of being asked before and I always said no because it just wasn't right. I was afraid that I would say no to Bill and not mean it. (girls!?) When I got home from that trip on the 15th, I started looking at wedding dresses, went to a French bakery in D.C., talked to a photographer, didn't sign anyone up but all the time thinking about being Bill's wife: Mrs. William Mc-Neice and move to California…hmmm. He didn't say anything about moving to Virginia…hmmm. Again, I thought, if I say no, that's it, I won't see him again, I'd have to live my life without him.

On the next trip, I said, "YES!" and told him about all the things that I had thought about and done while away from him, and he said, "You're looking at wedding dresses and I am pacing the floor wondering what I had done that you didn't want me!" Oh, it was so romantic.

But, during that week he had been looking at diamond rings at a special place in downtown L.A. Well, I had some vacation time off and went to see him in L.A., he took me to look at the diamonds that he had picked out. The man behind the counter (an older man with an older co-owner of the store) said to me, "Have you ever thought about what you would want in an engagement ring?" I said, "Yes, I want a round-solitaire-diamond-with-six-silver-prongs-in-a-gold-setting." Can you imagine a jeweler asking a 29-year-old maiden lady if she has ever thought about an engagement ring!?

It was beautiful! And it lasted a lifetime.

My Father walked me down the aisle of my church, Mt. Vernon Presbyterian Church just south of Alexandria, Virginia, November 30, 1974. Bill's parents came from Belfast and his sister and her family came from Toronto. My bride's maids were my two first cousins, Cathryn from Tulsa, Oklahoma and Betsy from Greenwood, Mississippi. I asked them if they had a long green dress, when they said yes, I said, wear them. They were beautiful. My Brother, Stan, was our best man. He was so handsome and proud of his role of best man.

While planning our wedding, I had called the National Symphony to ask if there was a harp student who knew some Irish music and would play at our wedding. The 1st Harpist, of the National Symphony, a lady, said she would be honored. She played so beautifully, I didn't want to miss it, so I opened the door of the bride's room where my Mother, Bill's mother, my brides' maids, and I listened. Bill's mother knew all the pieces the soloist had chosen to play and even sang along with a few.

I had asked the minister, Harry Jaeger, to invite the congregation to the wedding ceremony, many of them came and my Mother asked them to sit on the groom's side of the Church. Everyone was so loving and happy for us.

My dress was a dream come true, it was a Pricilla of Boston, creamy white with lace, pearls and a small train. The flowers that I carried were simple: three long-stem red roses, one that I gave to my Mother on the front row when Daddy walked me down the aisle, one for Bill's Mother that I gave to her as Bill and I walked together back up the aisle, and one for me.

Our reception was in Alexandria at "George Washington's Old Club," a historic favorite place of George Washington. I would say that about twenty of my Flight Attendant friends came to the wedding and reception, they were beautiful and so excited for us.

As in most protestant wedding receptions back then, the fare was simple: finger food (my parents having just returned from Hawaii, would have said "Heavy PuPu's" and a Champagne Fountain. The wedding cake was from a famous French Bakery in Washington, D.C. and had flowers on the top, I didn't want a "Bride and Groom" on the top. The bakery called me at 4:00 in the morning to ask me if I was sure that I wanted a hole on the top layer of the cake, and I reminded her again that the hole was for the vase of flowers.

Here is a funny story about the cake: remember that we didn't know each other very well. I was so proud of the cake that I had ordered with a swirl of different flavors in it and raspberry preserves between the layers. As Bill and I cut the cake, Bill was disappointed that it wasn't the fruitcake he was used to in Belfast. We laughed for years about the whispered words between us while we fed each other our first bite.

We had lots of pictures with family, church friends, my roommate from college, and Flight Attendants, it was so fun, but it was the last day of November and also the day of the Army-Navy Game, so some guests were running out to their cars to check on the score during the reception, and actually, my "garter" had a "Go Army" button on it!

But, it was cold outside and people were gathering to wave goodbye to us. I didn't take time to change into my "going away" outfit. We just got in the car, wedding dress and all. Bill had never driven my car, and didn't know where to go. A brilliant policeman showed up and asked Bill where he wanted to turn, I said a U-Turn, so the policeman stopped the traffic and we turned around heading into our new life. When we checked into the hotel, I got out of the car and went in with Bill, in my wedding dress, as I wanted to watch him write: Mr. and Mrs. William McNeice.

Bill (bottom, center) Covered with Flight Attendants

Bill and Tina November 30, 1974

Los Angeles — LAX

Flight 17

My transfer to Los Angeles was smooth in February 1975, and most of my trips were on the DC-10. Bill and I were getting used to our routine of my being gone three days a week and sometimes on weekends as I was not as senior in L.A. with only nine years with the company.

As a new family of two we wanted a different lifestyle that wasn't the single lifestyle, so while I was on my trips Bill started looking at houses in Orange County where he was selling more and more of his electronic test systems to the aerospace industry.

We found a house in the planned development community of Mission Viejo and moved in April 1975. Our new neighbors were wonderful and they had two little boys.

I felt so domestic with a house and a fireplace, a beautiful view, and a gorgeous husband. The carpet was already installed, so I got right to work ordering drapes and arranging our combined furniture. We now had a three- bedroom, two bath home with a separate dining room, living room, and family room. Our furniture fit just fine.

I ordered a "milk man." Oh, how times have changed and not just on the airplane. The milk man came once a week and brought milk, half and half in glass bottles, and sometimes cottage cheese. We found

95

someone to take care of our landscaping and funny enough, his name was "Mr. Green."

We needed a "family meeting." Growing up, when my Dad said we needed a family meeting, it usually meant we were going to move. Bill and I laughed that I wanted to talk: money.

I made a proposal: we had money, not all that much, but two incomes and we needed to handle it wisely. I don't know what Bill did before, he didn't say, I didn't ask. But what did he think about living on my income and investing his? He pays the mortgage, I pay for everything else. I received two paychecks a month, one larger than the other, Bill received commission checks from his sales every few months, in big chunks. We had one checking account and a growing savings account. When we gathered some money, we made our first investment in Public Storage II.

I remember thinking, when I first started flying in 1965, with my small but steady paychecks: I came from money but I don't have any; I need to start saving some of this every month. By the time we got married in 1974, I had a nice little savings account.

Not long after our family meeting, Bill, the engineer, sat me down to explain the "bell curve" to me because he wanted to double the mortgage payments every month. The mortgage payment was an investment and would be paid off sooner with higher early payments. We lived in that house 18 years and the mortgage was almost paid in full by the time we sold it in 1992.

This trip was a DC-10 from Los Angeles to Chicago, then on to Hartford, Connecticut and spend the night. After a nice trip from L.A. to Chicago, the weather from Chicago to Hartford was terrible. The Captain explained to the passengers that there would be no beverage service, and that the Flight Attendants would stay in their jumpseats for the whole trip. He was right, the turbulence was so bad my jumpseat almost closed under me, even with my seatbelt fastened. The cockpit crew later said the airplane was shaking so much they could hardly read the instruments.

We welcomed the sunshine the next morning as we prepared our flight from Hartford to New York's Kennedy Airport. Then we were going on to San Francisco; it was going to be a long day.

Among our passengers boarding in Hartford was an unaccompanied minor, Jeff, who was five years old. His grandmother brought him to the airplane and told us that he was going with us all the way to San Francisco and that his parents would meet us when we arrived. A very nice gentleman was seated next to Jeff. He was going to San Francisco too.

Our trip from Hartford to New York was smooth with no sign of the turbulence we had the evening before.

...TO SAN FRANCISCO

The agents wanted to start pre-boarding our passengers right away. Our special needs passengers included: five unaccompanied minors (one was our Jeff, five years old), mothers with 15 lap babies, and three totally incapacitated passengers brought on in seated gurneys. Two of these were traveling alone and seated on the aisle in coach. The other was in First Class traveling with his wife. All these passengers were part of our full load. Going from New York to San Francisco non-stop we were maxed out in fuel, so when our cockpit talked to the FAA tower we were called, "American Flt.17 Heavy." Our DC-10 had three engines, and 285 passengers.

This DC-10 had the latest equipment in the cockpit, including a camera behind the Captain's head looking across the cockpit and out of the front window. In each section of the airplane there was a big screen to show the movie that was planned for after the lunch service.

This is the screen where our passengers could watch the cockpit during take-off and landing. Part of our Flight Attendant procedures during boarding was to sell head-sets for the movie.

So, on this beautiful August 25, 1975, just after noon, the doors were closed for our trip to San Francisco. I was working in coach, Flight Attendant #6 in the back on the right-hand side, with my jump seat facing the aft coffee bar that had two coffee makers and two pre-positioned tray carts that were ready for the lunch service.

I had finished selling headsets on my side when the 1st Flight Attendant said over the P.A. system, "Prepare for departure," which was our signal that the boarding doors were closed and we were ready to leave the gate, I turned and "armed" my door by preparing the slide and door for an emergency.

I checked the passengers' seat belts in my area, then checked to see that the latches were secure on the carts in front of my jumpseat and checked that the coffee pots were locked in position. Then I sat down on my jumpseat and fastened my seat belt at door 4R with a lap full of headset money.

As we started our take-off roll it was easy to feel how heavy we were. The pilots pushed the power higher and higher, the plane lumbered a little as it started to pick up speed, faster and faster, powerful, loud, faster... faster... we were "haulin'!" Then, BANG!

What was that? We were haulin! Faster... Faster...

BANG!

"Those were tires!" I'm thinking. "We're going to have to stop this thing! And get out!"

I stuffed some headset money in my pockets and just threw the rest behind my jumpseat! The pilot started to abort the takeoff. He put all three engines in full reverse and was braking hard. One by one the other tires on the main landing gear were bursting, still braking hard with loud, loud engines in reverse. The vibration was incredible.

I tried to turn around from my jumpseat to look at the TV screen showing the cockpit. The crew members were stoic as we could only see their shoulders vibrating with the airplane trying to slow down. I wanted to see how close we were to the approaching landing lights at the end of the runway through the cockpit window. It was a really rough ride and hard to see down the runway from my position.

I put my legs straight out in front of me as well as my hands and arms, if those latches didn't hold those carts, I didn't want to get trapped against my jumpseat.

We stopped. I didn't know where we were but the airplane didn't break up, the overhead bins held shut, a few oxygen masks fell down, and some of the ceiling panels came down. Amazing! They didn't fall on our passengers as they were constrained by "bungee cords." No one had ever told us in training that the ceiling panels wouldn't or couldn't fall down.

We seemed to be at an angle, my side (right side) was higher, left wing low.

The Captain immediately made a P.A. "Use the right doors only and Easy Victor!"

I unfastened my seat belt and looked out the window in my door and looked out the passenger window beside my door. I didn't have any fire or smoke. I pushed up on the emergency door handle. As my door quickly slid up into the fuselage the slide deployed, unfolded and burst open just like the 747 slide inflated two years before, but this time the slide didn't settle at the proper angle. With my right side higher than the left side of the airplane, I could expect the angle to be steeper, but these slides are made extra-long for that. My slide just hung straight down.

What? There was no way my passengers could use this slide. If I didn't have that burst of power to inflate the slide, I could have pulled the red inflation handle. I couldn't believe it, but I didn't have time to debate what to do.

My slide was not usable and passengers were trying to go around me out the open door. I had my arms and hands out, across my door, "This exit blocked, turn around, go that way!" Across the plane on the left side, there was no fire or smoke, the door 4L was open and the Flight Attendant was calling the passengers to her door, "Unfasten seatbelts, come this way, remove shoes, don't take anything with you!"

There was fire outside of both over wing exits, and my slide was not useable; all the passengers in the back of the airplane had to exit through that aft left door. We didn't know it at the time, but the left engine was on fire and had partially come away from its pylon.

Passengers on the right side were throwing themselves across the five center seats trying to get to the left side. The two incapacitated passengers in different rows on the aisle, got up on their own, no help, held onto one seat back at a time, one foot in front of the other, and worked their way back to the useable exit. Other passengers weren't lined up behind them, they were jumping and climbing over the seats or going around them. I was still trying to protect the open door behind me with no slide. The good news is that the back slides are big enough to accommodate two at a time, side by side. Many tried to take carry-on items with them, and of course, the Flight Attendant was yelling, "Don't take anything with you!"

When the cabin was clear, I checked my area and made my way to the door at 4L, then jumped into the slide. As I was sliding down I was looking all around for Jeff, the five-year old, and there he was, holding the hand of the man that had been sitting next to him.

I ran to Jeff and threw my arms around him, hugging him, I said, "Jeff, Oh Jeff! How are you?" He said, "Did you see all the fire and the fire trucks?"

I noticed something on Jeff's wrist and asked, "Jeff what is that on your arm?" He said that it was his address and phone number. I thought, oh good, we can call his parents when we get inside the airport. All of the paperwork for our unaccompanied minors was under a clip in the First Class service center, the other children were old enough to know their phone numbers and other agents took care of them.

I asked the gentleman if he was okay and when he said yes, I asked if he would hold on to Jeff while I checked on the other passengers. It seemed like everyone was okay.

We didn't know it, but the tower timed us. The people working in the FAA tower managing take offs and landings saw our airplane blow the tires and the fire, and work at stopping the airplane, they knew we were going to have to evacuate. So when the airplane stopped and the first door opened, they timed us. We got everyone out only using four of the eight doors in 90 seconds with no injuries. I will say, later, we found out that a young man, traveling with his father, hit his head on the frame of the door where he was exiting. I don't know the outcome of that injury.

With all that fire and all that fuel, How in the world did we live through it?

BLUE SKIES SMILIN' AT ME

How in the world did we live through it? First, the plane held together. Second, the firemen and the fire trucks.

It had been raining in New York for three weeks straight and August 25th was the first beautiful, clear, sunny day. So the firemen were standing outside of the firehouse with their hands in their pockets watching airplanes take off and land.

When the firemen watched our "American Flight 17 Heavy" start our takeoff roll with full power on, they saw us blow the first tire. They jumped into action and into their fire trucks. They didn't wait to see what would happen next, they were putting on their equipment as they raced after our plane, saw the next tire blow, saw the engines go into reverse, full brakes applied, and then the fire started in the gear as the rest of the tires blew! The tires on the nose gear held.

Those firemen had foam on the airplane before we had the first door open.

I had mentioned two of the three incapacitated passengers got themselves out of the airplane grabbing one seat at a time. The third passenger was in First Class. Our procedures are: after other passengers are clear, we are to roll the passenger out of his/her seat onto the aisle floor and drag them by their feet to the exit door, then help them over the edge into the slide.

As our First Class F/As were dragging the passenger to the door, a fireman had managed to climb up another slide and yelled across First Class, "Stop! We'll get him out another way. The fire is out."

When we Flight Attendants got into the terminal building, we asked some agents about the unaccompanied children and we found Jeff. We took Jeff to a phone and I called his family using the phone number on his I.D. bracelet. Jeff's father answered the phone in California. When I said I was an American Airlines Flight Attendant on Jeff's flight to San Francisco, Jeff's father said they knew about the accident. Jeff's grandmother in Hartford had called to tell them. Jeff's mother had passed out, and a doctor was on his way to their house. "How's Jeff?" he asked. I said, "Fine, I'm going to let you speak to him." Jeff said, "Daddy, you should have seen all the fire and the fire trucks! Yes, I'm fine."

We informed his family that American would get back to them with the timing and arrangements to get Jeff home. We found the agent taking care of the unaccompanied minors and gave Jeff lots of hugs before turning him over to her.

Once we arrived at American's Operations, we were met by a supervisor and she said that we could call our families right after we wrote a report. They wanted a report while our experience was still fresh and we hadn't talked about it with others.

As soon as I finished my report, I gave it to the supervisor with the headset money from my pockets, then I found the Captain, Bill Deppy. I ran to him and gave him a big hug…he got lots of big hugs! We gathered around him and he explained:

"We weren't going to make the end of the runway, I could see that we were going to go through the approach (landing) lights and go into the water. I glanced to my left and saw a concrete wall at about 10 o'clock (a direction) and turned the nose gear to head for the concrete wall, I thought the people in the back of the airplane would live."

Only the Lord himself knew it had been raining for three weeks and when the Captain pulled off the runway toward the concrete wall, the nose gear went into the mud and stopped the airplane, right there.

I called my parents first, my Dad (the FAA man and pilot) and Mom said that Bill (my husband) had already called to tell them about our flight as American had notified him. I told my parents that American was going to have a hearing at 3:00 p.m., in about an hour. I would call them later.

I called Bill, (I've started some tears here)…He said, "American called, I was just leaving the house for a sales appointment but stopped when the phone rang. The woman said: 'Mr. McNeice? This is American Airlines, it's about your wife Tina.' "I said, yes, what about my wife, Tina?" 'She said, 'She has been in an accident at Kennedy Airport, but she's fine, everyone is fine. She will be calling you when she gets off the runway. We wanted to tell you before you see it on the news. If you have any questions, please call.'" He said, "OK, goodbye."

Bill said that he had lots of questions but wanted to turn on the television. And, there it was, the airplane leaning left side low, with the slides deployed and some fire trucks visible.

Then he called my parents. I told Bill that I would call him after the hearing.

American took our crew to a hotel very close to the airport where we had a preliminary hearing with the Chief Pilot for American, the Chief Pilot at Kennedy, Flight Attendant Supervisors, maintenance supervisors, and other managers that could be there in a short amount of time.

Each crew member spoke about his or her experience on the airplane. This is when we found out that it was the Co-Pilot's leg to fly us to San Francisco. This is not unusual, the Co-Pilots take turns with the Captain about every-other leg to take off and land the airplane.

Our Co-Pilot reported: With his left hand pushing forward on the throttles, full power on, the right hand holding the yolk (steering wheel), the airplane going faster and faster, they heard something, faster and faster, the "pilot-not-flying" (Captain) called out the speed of the plane. Except just as the Captain said rotate (lift off the runway), there was another Bang!

The Co-Pilot pulled the throttles back, slamming the brakes hard.

The Captain said, "I've got it." helped slam on the brakes. This is when the Captain took over (these are procedures they practice with all their training twice a year).

It was at this point the Captain could tell that we were going off the end of the runway and decided to pull off to the left and saved us when the nose gear went in the mud.

The Captain's side of the cockpit has the wheel that controls the nose gear and directs the plane on the ground.

During the hearing, it was amazing to be there when the Chief Pilots ask the questions, discussing at length the details of what went on in the cockpit.

Each F/A had to give a report of her experience (there were no male Flight Attendants on this trip). JFK Flight Attendant supervisors and training supervisors asked us questions. A Flight Attendant supervisor asked me if I pulled the red inflation handle when it was clear that my slide had not fully inflated? I told her no, as I had such a big burst of CO_2 when the slide deployed and unfolded that I was sure the CO_2 was depleted. She didn't ask me any more questions.

Here, I want to say that, in December of that year, 1975, at a meeting for 1st Flight Attendants at my base in Los Angeles, two maintenance men, one was a supervisor, came into the meeting and asked for me. They took me aside and said they wanted to tell me that my slide at 4R from the Flight 17 accident had been scrutinized and tested and the CO_2 had fully deployed to its capacity but the slide had a leak and did not hold at the proper angle. If I had taken the time to pull the "red handle" nothing would have happened. I did the right thing by redirecting the passengers away from the open door immediately. What a relief! This gave me closure that my instincts were correct.

At the close of this hearing near the airport, American told us there would be an FAA hearing at the same location in the morning at 9:00. American had made arrangements for our crew to stay at the Sheraton Americana downtown, with a limo pick-up at 8:00 a.m. We could make all the calls we wanted to and any room service was on American. In the limo into town, the Captain said he wanted us to be in uniform for the FAA hearing and to meet in the lobby a little before 8:00 a.m.

I need to explain that the "limo" was really a bus, to fit all of us for the ride to and from town. The word limo was used back in the 1940s and '50s, when the crew was transported in limousines, and they all fit into one vehicle.

After we arrived at the hotel, most of us went out to dinner so we could have a drink and walk off some stress.

I called Bill when I got back to the room and told him about the hearing and more details about the accident. My roommate (we were still sharing rooms) called her family. Then I called my parents again and told them about American's hearing and much about what the pilots said and did in the cockpit. I also told them (Mother on one phone, Dad on the other, we always talked that way) that the FAA hearing was going to be at 9:00 in the morning and our limo pick-up was at 8:00. I asked my Dad (retired from the FAA one year) if there was anything special I should say in the hearing? He said to report everything just as it happened and you'll do just fine. I told them that I would call them as soon as I could after the hearing, but to not wait on my call.

Mother and Daddy already had their car packed as they were leaving early in the morning to drive from Ft. Myers, Florida to California to visit us and to see our new house. My brother was visiting a friend from high school in Lake Tahoe, Nevada and we were planning to gather at our house in Southern California for a family visit before Stan left for his next base assignment in Korea.

ONWARD CHRISTIAN SOLDIERS

As a crew, as a group, as individuals, we couldn't sleep. We don't know what the Pilots did, but we F/As all had our doors open most of the night: we checked our flashlights, we checked our manuals to make sure our revisions were up to date, we walked from room to room, we sat down on the floor in the hall, we talked, and we laughed. Much of this was the stress of what we had just been through together, it was another way of holding hands. Perhaps it was group PTSD (Post Traumatic Stress Disorder), which we had never heard of in 1975. But, then, we didn't know what to expect at the FAA hearing and we were nervous wrecks!

We did close our doors and settled down, it was late and I don't think I slept. So, my roommate and I were up early, showered, dressed in our uniforms, ordered room service, opened the door to our room and found that everybody else was up with their doors open and waiting for room service too.

The phone rang. I answered it...it was my Mom! The other phone at home didn't pick up. She said, "Sister, are you alone?" I told her we were all up with our doors open and waiting for room service.

She said, "Are you sitting down?" I realized she was serious. I said, "Yes." She said, "Our Daddy just died."

WHAT!?

It was like I was evacuating again, I was in full emergency mode....

"Mother, are you alright? Where are you? Are you alone? What happened? Is Barbara with you? (neighbor). Where's Stan?"

She told me: In his sleep, Daddy tried to stop that airplane all night long.

They were up early to have coffee and eat before getting in the car to leave for California. They were still in the kitchen, Daddy was sitting at the table smoking a cigarette, Mother was standing facing him at the sink smoking a cigarette and talking to him. He gave a little cough and started falling forward, she threw her cigarette in the sink, grabbed his cigarette, threw it in the sink and had her hands under his head before it hit the floor.

My Dad was 58, my Mom, 53.

She immediately started mouth-to-mouth resuscitation (she didn't know CPR). In a couple of minutes, she sat up and said to my Dad, "Sweetheart, nobody knows we need help. I'll be right back." A neighbor was outside tending to his garden. She said to him, "Hayward is sick, call an ambulance, tell them to bring oxygen."

She went back to mouth-to-mouth. Mother said in just minutes someone picked her up by the elbows and said, "We'll take over now,

Ma'am." She told me she said, "Then, if you'll excuse me," (she was forever the Southern lady) "I'll change my clothes to go with you in the ambulance."

The man looked up and said, "Ma'am, you don't need to change your clothes." She said "Oh, then I have to call my daughter in New York, before she leaves the hotel!"

While I was talking to my Mom, I whispered to my roommate, "My Dad just died." She found our 1st Flight Attendant and told her. She contacted the Captain.

My mother was so strong and "had her head on straight," she said she had several people she needed to talk to, including my brother. I told her that I didn't know how fast I could get to her in Ft. Myers, that the hearing might take several hours. She said she had lots of help and things to do. "I'll be fine, Sister, take care of yourself."

When I saw the Captain in the lobby, he came right to me and held me, then he said, "Your Dad was our only fatality."

Everyone was very caring.

When we got to the hearing, the head of Flight Attendant training, Kay Avery, from Headquarters, in Ft. Worth, came to me and hugged me and said that I didn't have to testify, but to tell her everything that I did and experienced and she would represent me. We talked in a room by ourselves. Then I asked her if I could call Bill. She said by all means and that a Kennedy Flight Attendant Supervisor was coming to take me to the airport and put me on an Eastern Airlines flight to Ft. Myers.

Bill was shocked and very worried about me. I told him I was OK and needed to just keep going. The Supervisor arrived to take me to the airport. I told Bill I would stay in touch and American would help him with plans to get to Ft. Myers.

The Supervisor took me to the gate at Eastern Airlines, then on to the airplane and sat me down in the First-Class seat. She took the

Eastern Flight Attendants aside and explained why I was still in my uniform and about the accident they had all heard about the day before, and my Dad.

When the AA Supervisor left, the First Flight Attendant came to me and held my hand. The Eastern Pilots arrived and seeing me in uniform in the front row of First Class, the Captain said, "Hey, is that American? You weren't in that accident yesterday, were you?" The Flight Attendant turned and hustled them up into the cockpit and explained my presence on their airplane. The Captain came out and gave me a hug.

Mother was so strong. She had called their lawyer, the funeral home, their church in Ft. Myers, Mt. Vernon Presbyterian Church in Alexandria, and several close friends. She wanted to stay busy, but she also wanted to get lots of things done before Stan, Bill, and I got there.

Mother's good friend and neighbor, Barbara Damiano took her to Page Field in Ft. Myers to pick me up. Stan and Bill arrived the next day, on the 27th.

I contacted Culpeper National Cemetery in Culpeper, Virginia, to see if we could make arrangements to have Dad buried there. Culpeper said yes, there was space next to the Flag Pole.

There was a small but beautiful service at the funeral home in Ft. Myers. My parents' new friends and neighbors of only one year were so loving and understanding. Then we flew with Daddy's body to Washington's National Airport and stayed with our family's life-long dear old friends, near our church in Alexandria. Relatives arrived from Oklahoma and Mississippi. They had just been there for our wedding less than a year ago. Everyone was in shock.

The service at Mt. Vernon Presbyterian Church was standing room only and the choir loft was packed with choir members who had been in Daddy's choir for years. They came to participate even if they had moved on to another church choir.

The music was incredible.

We sang the hymns: "Joyful Joyful, We Adore Thee" and "Abide With Me."

The choir sang: "The King of Love My Shepherd Is," "Jesu, Priceless Treasure," and "The Hallelujah Chorus."

GOING HOME

Bill had to bring clothes for me to wear to the funeral in Alexandria, as all I had with me were clothes for my three-day trip with the layover in Hartford which already seemed like a month ago.

It was comforting to stay with these old family friends, but before the funeral service at the church, I went off by myself, used their home phone, and called a doctor who had treated me for some digestion problems and weight loss. In fact, he put me in the hospital twice, this is before I met Bill and when I was still based in D.C. I told the doctor about the accident, which he had seen in the news reports, and I told him about my Dad.

My question was coping without making myself sick, and no, I wasn't going to see him, he would put me in the hospital! And no, no medicine. He said to sit quietly in a room by myself with very little light and just be alone for a while.

In some ways I felt selfish as, in my mind, I was still evacuating that airplane, and I couldn't stop. Having my family together and near me was probably the best thing for me and the best thing for all of us.

I didn't cry. The Hallelujah Chorus was tough, but, then, somewhere I found an inner peace and an inner strength. Mom was strong, Stan was strong. Bill was strong.

We got through it and we "soldiered on."

"Going Home" is the standard tune played on Bagpipes or sung at a funeral in Scotland. We didn't have "Going Home" for our Dad's funeral, but driving from Alexandria to Culpeper National Cemetery, through Virginia was like going home. It was amazing how many people drove with us all that way; it probably took two hours. Family members, FAA men, and my Dad's former secretary from the D.C. office, neighbors from my parents' house South of Mt. Vernon where they lived before they moved to Hawaii and Florida, along with lots of friends from the church all arrived at the same time at the beautiful National Cemetery.

On a hill, my Dad is right next to the Flag Pole.

Hayward S. Florer Dies; Ex-FAA Safety Expert

Hayward S. Florer, 58, a retired safety expert with the Federal Aviation Administration, died Tuesday in Fort Myers, Fla., after apparently suffering a heart attack.

HAYWARD S. FLORER

He had lived in Fort Myers since retiring last year although he still maintained a home in Sulgrave Manor, Fairfax County.

Born in Terlton, Okla., Mr. Florer graduated from Central State University in Edmond and taught in the Oklahoma public school system prior to World War II.

During the war, he was a pilot with the Army Air Corps Ferry Command, transporting fighters and bombers to Europe, Africa and the Far East.

In 1946, he joined the Civil Aeronautics Administration, predecessor of the FAA, and was first assigned as an air carrier inspector at LaGuardia Airport in New York.

After a year there, he came to Washington to the Flight Safety Regulations Division, continuing in that position with the FAA, after it was established in 1958. He had spent two years during that time with the Flight Standards Division at Fort Worth, Texas.

From 1962 to 1972, Mr. Florer was assistant division chief of the FAA safety regulation staff here. For the next two years, until his retirement in 1974, he was chief of the Flight Standards Division of the FAA in Honolulu.

Mr. Florer was one of the founders, an elder and the first choir director of Mount Vernon Presbyterian Church here and later a member of the choir of Faith United Presbyterian Church in Cape Coral, Fla.

He was a major in the Air Force Reserve and belonged to the National Association of Retired Federal Employees.

He is survived by his wife, Amelia (Mimi) Florer, of the home in Fort Myers; a daughter, Amelia Justina McNeice of Mission Viejo, Calif.; a son, 1st Lt. Hayward S. Jr., attached to the 82d Airborne Division, and a sister, Agnes Schellstede, of Tulsa, Okla.

The family suggests that expressions of sympathy be in the form of contributions to memorial fund at Mount Vernon Presbyterian Church Alexandria.

From the Washington Post

The Green Berets

My brother was stationed in Korea for 13 months, then he went back to his last base in Ft. Bragg in North Carolina. There is no "rest for the weary" when it comes to our military. He was already Airborne qualified and Ranger qualified before he went to Korea, so he started right in to more training. Then, he was sent to the Special Forces unit in Bad Tolz, West Germany. He had been given no language school for German, he went in cold.

Now my brother is not shy, shortly after he got settled into his new base he explored Bad Tolz. Then one night he went to a bar for dinner and ordered whatever the guy next to him was drinking.

I can't say they struck up a conversation because that guy didn't speak English and Stan didn't speak German. Stan went to that bar every night and listened, learned, and tried words and hand signals, and found out these guys were police officers and, in no time, he had some friends.

As he became more comfortable with his German language, on "days off," he went up to Munich and joined a Rugby team in order to make more friends who were athletic and in shape. He also learned Rugby songs. There is a very interesting culture with Rugby teams in Germany.

Now that my brother was in Germany we wanted to go to see him. So did Mother.

Did I tell you that Mother moved to California to be near us?

We went to Ft. Myers to visit her several times, but she came to California to visit us too. Then she came too often and stayed too long, so Bill did some research and found a house in Mission Viejo's over 55 community called Casta Del Sol. It was only three miles away from our house.

With Mother's charming Southern accent and demeanor, she had a "Gentleman Caller" in no time. Bill liked that, it kept her busy.

Mother and I started taking German language classes at Saddleback Community College, as we wanted to be able to get around in Germany without being dependent on Stan. Bill studied German in books, there were no computers yet. He did very well ("I'm an Engineer, you know"), but he didn't have a chance to speak it in a classroom. His vocabulary grew and grew without the class.

The three of us studied German the whole four and a half years Stan was in Germany.

Bad Tolz is a beautiful town in Southern Germany, about 40 miles south of Munich. It is a well-known resort because of its natural Springs.

Our first visit was in November, for Thanksgiving. Bill and I flew separately from Mother as we stopped in Holland for a few days to visit friends from Bill's work with N.V. Philips.

Bill and I had rented a car and met Mother in Munich. We were all excited about staying in my brother's apartment and meeting his roommate who was another Special Forces Captain. He was the Battalion Surgeon while he was based in Bad Tolz.

They were ready for a Thanksgiving dinner.

The day before Thanksgiving we bought a turkey and all the fixings at the commissary on the Kaserne. Also, that day Bad Tolz was having what we would call a "Farmers' Market" in town. Mother, Bill, and I strolled the market when all of a sudden Mother said, "I need bananas for the fruit salad." Then she asked Bill, "How do you say six bananas?"

Bill said, "sechs banane. Say it like sex bananan."

She went over to the fruit stand and we could hear her say to the farmer, "sieben bananan." She paid for her seven bananas. When she came back to us, I asked her why she said seven bananas, when she wanted six.

She said, "I couldn't say sex to that man."

Another 747 Story

At home, in Mission Viejo, out of the clear blue, Bill said, "We need a new car, my car embarrassed me again today." I asked him what happened? He said the car wouldn't start and a customer was in the car. He had to call AAA to get a jump start and then he had to buy a new battery.

He was a little hesitant when he said, "I want a car I can depend on, what do you think about a Mercedes Benz?"

Without missing a beat I said, "OK, one of our Pilots is selling Mercedes and we could buy one through him with an airline discount!"

Here's the story:

I was still flying to Hawaii out of LAX and during dinner one night in Honolulu, with lots of members of our crew, one of the Pilots told us he was representing Mercedes Benz and he could sell cars to crew members at a discount. The stipulation was that crew members had to take delivery at the factory in Sindelfingen, West Germany and could get an airline discount shipping the car home.

When I told Bill this news, Bill called him and they made a deal. It was good for everybody and Bill couldn't believe the timing was so perfect.

In April 1982, Bill and I flew to Frankfurt, West Germany on Lufthansa Airlines, we rented a car and spent the night. In the morning, we drove to the Mercedes Benz factory in Sindelfingen. After we checked in we were told that they would take care of our rental car. Then we were invited to have a tour of the factory. When the tour was over, a Mercedes engineer who spoke perfect English was assigned to us and he explained every detail of our car.

Our 300SD was especially made with California specifications, that was for emission standards, and the dashboard was for an American car in mileage not kilometers.

Part of this briefing was to say that the car had a full tank of diesel fuel and that they wanted us to drive the car at least 50 miles before we shipped it to America. That mileage was to make sure we were familiar with everything and that the fluids were settled. Then he helped us with the delivery paperwork, which was just a signature.

Our car was beautiful, a dream come true, and Bill was beside himself he was so happy and proud. We had it all planned to drive to Bad Tolz to show our car to my brother.

The next morning, in the car before starting our ride to Bad Tolz, Bill surprised me with a present for our car, a CD of Pachelbel's Canon in D Major. We had a CD player and nothing could be more perfect for our Mercedes in Germany than Pachelbel's Canon. It became "our song."

The Autobahn was scary and we weren't supposed to drive fast yet (part of our instructions: stay in the slow lane). Finally, we arrived in Bad Tolz and my brother was really impressed, he had just bought a BMW 320i sedan, which he loved and yes, it was beautiful too, but nothing measured up to our baby. We only spent one night with my brother, but overnight it snowed, it snowed on our new car, with no carport or garage. We couldn't wait to take it home to California.

Part of the plan with the Pilot who was our dealer was that we had to "take delivery" of two Porsches at the Porsche factory in Stuttgart. Upon our arrival at the factory, we were invited to have a tour. The tours of these factories were just incredible and the tour guides spoke the languages of everyone in the tour, amazing.

To take delivery of the Porsches, we had to look over the first car inside and out, then sign for it, then look over the second car and sign for it. Then the cars would be put on a ship and delivered to the East Coast of the United States.

The plan for shipping our car was different. We shipped our car by cargo on Lufthansa with an airline discount. The instructions we had been given were that we take the car to the Frankfurt Airport at Lufthansa's Cargo drop off point and the car had to be just about out of fuel when we dropped it off.

The Lufthansa agent that met us was expecting us. He inspected the car, as we could have nothing in it, no personal belongings, no luggage, empty.

We asked him when he thought our car might make the trip as it would be on stand-by. He looked at his watch and said, it will probably be on the 1:30 to Los Angeles today. We were in shock, that was our flight! How could that be? He said the Lufthansa airplane was a "747 Combi" and was equipped to handle passengers and cargo.

We were excited and nervous on the jet bridge boarding the airplane. The Purser was at the boarding door and I asked her, "Do you know if there is a new Mercedes on board?" She lit up and said, "Yes, a silver one." I said, "That's our car!"

Well, I gave birth to that car on take-off. I didn't know how it was strapped down. Did they put on the parking brake? Would it be positioned facing forward or aft or sideways? Was everything around it tied down well? I wanted to sit next to it, Bill was almost the same way.

We were so excited, we told the man sitting next to us about the car. We were in coach with three seats together and he caught our excitement right away. He asked us lots of questions about the car and the deal. He was fascinated.

After the lunch service, while the movie was showing, the Purser came to our seats and asked if we would like to go see our car. Are you kidding? And, she asked, would the man sitting with us like to go too? Can you imagine? The Purser unlocked the door behind the last row of seats in coach, and there was our new silver Mercedes facing forward with no other cargo or suitcases around it. We opened the doors to show the Purser and our new friend the interior. The seats were a light silver-gray, the plush carpet and the rest of the interior was a darker gray color. Details of the dash board and bucket seat divider were a dark walnut. What an experience! Then I was calm, our baby was fine, and safe.

It was after 4:00 p.m. in Los Angeles when we landed and customs for cargo was closed so we couldn't drive the car home that night. We rented a car to go home and it was convenient to bring it back when we picked up our pride and joy in the morning.

Bill with New 1982 Mercedes Benz 300SD

Change of Command

As a Major, my brother was selected to go to the Command and General Staff College (CGSC) in Ft. Leavenworth, Kansas. While he was there, he met his future wife, Patty, a beautiful, educated lady from Missouri. He also completed his Master's degree in history from the University of Kansas in a program offered by the CGSC.

They were married in the Seventh Cavalry Memorial Chapel at Ft. Leavenworth. Mother, Bill, and I were able to be there for their perfect wedding on a gorgeous day in October.

Their first assignment together was to the Defense Language School in Monterrey, California. They both studied French for six months.

I continued to fly from LAX to HNL.

After five very busy years, Patty gave birth to a beautiful baby girl, whom I call "Sister." Oh, what a new baby does to a family!

Special Forces moved them to Patrick Air Force Base near Melbourne, Florida.

Bill and I visited them a couple of times in Florida from California and enjoyed the weather, exotic birds, and this growing cherub. On different trips, we watched Sister begin to crawl, stand up for the first time, and to tell us to "chew, chew, chew, swallow, swallow, swallow".

Still based at Patrick AFB, they took Sister to headquarters and introduced her to his commanding officer and said that he was a helicopter pilot. Sister said, "Ooh, 'copter, careful."

After Patrick Air Force Base, my brother was sent back to Bad Tolz, West Germany, this time with his family. He honored Bill and me with an invitation to his "Change of Command" ceremony to assume command of the Special Forces Battalion there.

We were comfortable taking care of their daughter while Stan and Patty attended the receiving line and reception in their honor.

At one point when we were outside of the reception hall, Sister started walking up a small hill and turned back to Uncle Bill (who was following her) and said, "Ocean?" She was wondering if the ocean was over the hill. Patrick Air Force Base was on the Atlantic Ocean, where is the ocean now?

Mother, Bill, and I started taking German again.

The next time we visited them in Bad Tolz, Sister knew the area. When we were out in the car, Sister would say from the booster seat behind Bill: "Turn here, Uncle Bill!" She was always right, amazing how that child knew where she was and how to get where we were going!

So Bill would say (after he turned with her directions): "Sister, put a sock in it!" teasing, meaning, "Sister, be quiet." She would snap back: "Chill out, Uncle Bill." Bill loved it. So did Sister.

Stan's next assignment was the "War College Fellowship" at Ft. Leavenworth, Kansas. During this busy time, Sam was born in Kansas City. This bundle of joy has grown up to be a 6'3" history expert giving tours at the Confederate White House in Richmond, as well as out in the battlefields of Virginia. Sam has earned his Bachelors and Masters degrees in History from William and Mary in Williamsburg, Virginia.

Our family is so proud.

Aloha Oe

American began flying to Honolulu, Hawaii (HNL) from Los Ange-
les in 1980 on the Boeing 747. I was excited to take the special training
at Flagship University in Ft. Worth to be over-water qualified for International flights.

Training for International included much more paperwork and procedures, but the big difference was the "over-water" part. American has
an indoor swimming pool in one building of the training center set up
with an airplane wing over part of the pool. The "wing" is the jumping off
point for us to get into the water and swim to or tread water to the slide-
life raft that some instructors had thrown in the water near the wing.

Our challenge during this part of training is to get into the raft
after jumping off the wing. There are rope-like fabric lines about two
inches wide along the inside and outside of the raft with a fabric "step"
for us to put our foot into at one end of the raft. We grab the line running along the outside and pull ourselves up, into the raft.

Some of our Flight Attendants didn't know how to swim. Think of
how brave those F/As were to take this training to qualify for flying
International flights. We that could swim "had their back." They had
to accomplish this climb into the raft by themselves, but knowing they
had help close by gave them confidence.

When you hear that a plane is equipped for over-water, it's not just the "life vest under your seat." Those airplanes have special equipment packed in the slides and in the extra rafts in the ceiling. It's amazing, this is in each slide:

1. sea anchor—fabric, looks like a wind sock, keeps the raft from spinning and keeps the raft closer to the location for a rescue
2. canopy and poles—for protection from the sun and elements, it can completely enclose the raft for warmth.
3. repair clamps—for surface of raft
4. position lights
5. life lines—to tie rafts together and trailing for someone in the water trying to get to the raft
6. oars
7. bailing bucket—fabric with an adjustable wire to make it a bucket
8. signaling mirror
9. flashlight
10. police whistle
11. dye marker
12. compass
13. water/food rations think: granola bar or trail mix without peanuts
14. de-salinization kit for treating sea water
15. survival kit—think: first aid kit with bandages and band aids, sunscreen, eye ointment, seasickness pills

These are 10 to 12-person life-rafts that can over load with a few more or some can hold on to the fabric lines around the outside until other rafts can tie together.

Flying time from LAX to HNL was about six hours going over and five hours coming back. When we started flying to Hawaii, smoking was still allowed and it wasn't a divided cabin of smoking and no smoking. Passengers could even smoke in the lavatories.

Our layover in Honolulu was at the Sheraton Americana Hotel and it was beautiful.

The trip I want to tell you about was in November of 1982. The airplane was a Boeing 747 with a full load of passengers. We signed-in for our trip in operations, and we were told to see the Captain, which is a little unusual as the 1st Flight Attendant is the one that reports to him. I was not 1st Flight Attendant on this trip as my seniority was too low (1st Flight Attendants had a separate seniority list), so I worked in coach. No problem, I loved it.

The Captain, who was very senior and was going to retire in a couple of months, told us that there was a hurricane headed toward Honolulu and American's Operations was trying to figure out the timing of our trip and the arrival of "IWA," the name of the hurricane.

American notified the passengers that we were delayed because of weather in HNL. But then we got the word that IWA was going to miss Honolulu and we could board the passengers right away. The passengers' luggage had already been boarded. Soon we were ready to go.

Our trip went smoothly with the beverage service, then the lunch service, then the movie, in fact, we showed two movies. But, during the second movie, the 1st F/A called all 14 Flight Attendants to the First Class service center to tell us that Hurricane IWA had turned toward Honolulu. We had passed the half-way point, the point of no return, and it looked like the hurricane and our flight would arrive at the same time. We couldn't get there ahead of the storm, and we couldn't slow down for it to pass (fuel).

When the second movie was over we served a light meal and beverage service, then we all worked at making sure that everything we saw was contained and locked down. You have never seen checking seatbelts with such attention. And mothers with lap babies were briefed about holding on to the baby. Babies can't be strapped in with the mother's seatbelt as the baby can be injured, as strong as the mother's arms can be, there is still enough give to be safe. This was going to be an amazing landing.

The Captain told the passengers about the change in the weather and that he wanted the Flight Attendants to check the cabin and take our jumpseats early as the turbulence could start any time and it could be rough.

Hold on:

The hurricane was moving into Honolulu straight across the run-way, lining up a normal approach glide path wouldn't work, so this is what our brilliant Captain did: In a very wide circle, descending but with full power on, he took us North—West of the airport over the mountains, then descending straight into the hurricane strength wind, heading South, we were perpendicular to the runway. He timed it per-fectly so that we descended right down to the end of the runway, then he kicked the rudder to turn us left, the airplane reacted (Boeing-747!) on a dime and we were on the ground.

Stay with me: now we've got to stop this thing!!

To give the pilots and airplane more control, we were still with full power on, now, on the ground, he put all four engines in full reverse, braking hard. Our great big vertical stabilizer (upright tail) was now a weather vane taking full brunt of Hurricane IWA. The wings were moving up and down in the wind and horizontal rain.

As I was sitting on my jumpseat and looking out the window, feel-ing the airplane vibrate and shake trying to stop, I saw a building blow across the runway in front of our plane. Later the Captain said the tower radioed: "American, do you see the hangar blowing across in front of you?" And, our Co-Pilot pressed his microphone to the tower and simply said: "Roger."

We were on an extra-long runway, both because it would give us a longer distance to stop the airplane in the storm and because we were a 747 and needed a longer runway anyway. This extra-long runway was the newly finished in 1977 "Reef" runway that was an alternate runway for the Space Shuttle. Five alternate runways had been built for the Space Shuttle around the world in case of an emergency. We were fortunate that it was there for us.

We stopped. The tires held. Our engines were champions and saved us. We lumbered to the terminal building slowly as the hurricane didn't stop just because we were on the ground. In the terminal building the wind had blown in one of the big glass windows at a gate full of people. Several people were hurt and being tended to by American's gate agents until help could arrive. It was serious.

Our passengers were shaken but did fine. They didn't know what was ahead of them getting to their destination, whether it was a hotel or home. Vacation?

And, all the power was out.

And, the next day was Thanksgiving.

The Sheraton Americana sure looked good even with no power, lights, elevators, or food. We had to carry our suitcases up the seven flights of stairs in a staircase with only emergency lights. After changing our clothes, we gathered back down in the lobby to continue to pat the Captain and cockpit crew on the back and sooth each other's nerves. We found out that the city was going to be able to have rolling electricity and people could cook their turkeys during the three hours of electricity in their area. We ate mostly junk food from the convenience store in the lobby. I believe we were delayed two days before we were able to go home to Los Angeles.

We missed Thanksgiving at home. Hurricane IWA left a lasting impression on all of us.

I flew to Hawaii seven times a month for five years.

Dallas

England and Germany

In the Spring of 1985, American decided to start flying international flights out of our headquarters hub in Dallas. The first flights were to England's Gatwick Airport near London. Then Frankfurt was added.

I wanted to fly to Europe and I had already qualified to work "over water" by training to fly to Hawaii.

The transfer to Dallas went smoothly. My seniority was pretty good with just about twenty years. I flew to Dallas the day before my trips and stayed in a hotel in order to be rested for my flights to England. I didn't get an apartment as I didn't want to divide my life, I wanted to go home after my trips. I slept the three hours flying back to California. I commuted between Los Angles and Dallas for eight years.

There was more training for international: more paperwork, different P.A.s (public address announcements), customs forms, duty free money to turn in. Now I changed from First Flight Attendant to "Purser." It meant more money, but also more training, meetings, and responsibility.

Flying to London's Gatwick Airport was wonderful and in the Spring, seeing the mustard fields was amazing. It was a couple of years before we added Heathrow to our England destinations. But I was anxious to fly to Frankfurt to see how I could get along with my new language skill. I did fine in Bavaria and now this would be business and formal.

The trips we fly, both domestic and international, are determined by our seniority. Every month we are given a "bid sheet" with the schedule and destination(s) listed with our choices from which to choose. On the given day that "bids" are due, Flight Attendants submit a list in order of their desires and are awarded their choice in order of seniority. If we want to change a trip for some reason, we can "trip trade" with another Flight Attendant (or Purser).

Our international flights had a qualified "speaker of destination" in each cabin on the airplane. Once our passengers in First Class knew that I was not the German "speaker," I started a few words and then more of a conversation...conversation? Maybe not. But I did fine, and I loved it.

Germans are very patient when you try to speak their language.

We stayed downtown in Frankfurt, by the Main River, it was beautiful. We shopped and took tours and found wonderful restaurants and museums. It was like a 24-hour vacation with little or no sleep.

The only English-speaking television station at that time was an American military station, Armed Forces Network. We could get news and some sports which were great company in the middle of the night when we couldn't sleep. Eventually we learned more about resting on these layovers: no need to watch TV, or pace the floor, or walk up and down the hall, or cry, or read all night. Like I said before, with no lights, or TV, I closed my eyes and was quiet. My body rested.

American did some research in finding a less expensive location for us to stay. Our trip was no longer just out of Dallas. We added Chicago, New York, and Boston. That required more and more hotel rooms and limos. So, we stayed in Mainz, on the Rhine River, then Darmstadt, then back to Mainz. These cities were/are close to the Frankfurt Airport and gave us a wonderful experience in Germany.

Let me tell you about some flights to and from Germany.

This flight stands out, and again, it was a medically tainted problem from Dallas to Frankfurt. After the service, and after Duty Free, during the dark, quiet time of the movie, a man's wife got the attention of a Flight Attendant in coach to say that her husband was having chest pains and he was short of breath. While the Flight Attendant made a P.A. call asking for a doctor, another Flight Attendant took an oxygen bottle to the passenger's seat. A doctor quickly responded to the call. After the doctor spoke to the passenger, he reported to us that the man with chest pains was also a doctor, he knew what was wrong and what he needed. Having this young doctor to talk with and having the oxygen relaxed the passenger. He was peaceful sitting with the oxygen; we checked on him often. He went to sleep.

First Class was almost empty, so we invited the young doctor to sit in First Class and have a drink for a few minutes. We wanted to hear his story. Yes, he was a medical doctor, from Germany, but his specialty was research and he had been invited to study and teach at three different university research labs in the United States. This trip, his first to the United States, had been to visit these universities and to decide where he wanted to go.

We asked him what he thought. You could tell he was excited to talk to us. I will always remember what he said: "The first thing I have to say is that I didn't realize how hard Americans work. I am an educated man but I guess I always thought that wealth and prosperity and advantages just came to Americans. Now I know it's because Americans work hard. Americans work hard and innovate. They try to figure out a better way to do things, not an easier way, a better way."

WOW, we Flight Attendants just looked at each other.

Then he said, "And I am amazed at the quality of these universities' research labs. They are all excellent, in fact, it is hard to choose which one to accept."

We asked what his choices were and he said, "Columbia in New York City, University of Iowa in Iowa City, Iowa, and Stanford, near Palo Alto, California." We asked him if there were any other influences to help him make up his mind? Did he want to get married? Did he want big city or beautiful countryside, or mountains for skiing? Then he added, "I think I will go to Columbia, in New York. After all, New York is the capitol of the world."

… Paris in the Springtime

Flying to Paris was absolutely a dream come true. It is everything wonderful that you have ever heard.

The French cuisine and restaurants are worth the trip if for no other reason. The museums, art, cathedrals, and the Eiffel Tower are on show every minute. I have never been anywhere that is such a delight to just walk, for hours, like Paris. And that is, year-round. The River Boat tour on the Seine River is a must. You will feel like you are in the Audrey Hepburn and Cary Grant movie "Charade."

Speaking of Audrey Hepburn, I feel like she raised me as I followed her through every movie on and off the screen. She started taking ballet when she was five years old and she was such a lady.

On one trip to Paris I found out that there was going to be a tribute to Audrey Hepburn by Hubert de Givenchy on the day we were in Paris, and the public was invited. It was a presentation of the clothes he had designed for her in her movies. I couldn't call them costumes. They were her clothes and they were exquisite. I loved all her clothes and Givenchy's designs set the style of that era. It was "the look." All the clothes I bought had to have the look, or style, of Hubert de Givenchy and Audrey Hepburn.

Three of us went to that presentation. It was beautiful, and I couldn't believe that I had been so fortunate to be there to participate in that tribute, maybe you could call it a worship service.

I took French during my freshman year in college and learned some phrases, greetings, and how to say, "thank you" and "excuse me." Other than that, nothing much I could use on the airplane.

Bill was proficient in the French language ("I'm an Engineer you know"), so I asked him to teach me a couple of useful phrases for the airplane. I thought: "Where is the bathroom?" and the answer: "The bathroom is in the back." Would be helpful in coach. I remember to this day practicing "Ou est la toilette?" and "La toilette est al'arriere."

On the airplane, preparing for boarding on my first trip to Paris, I was working in Business Class. I told the Business Class Galley Flight Attendant who was also the Business Class French Speaker about my new language skill, he laughed. The timing was perfect as we heard the Purser say over the P.A. "We're boarding!" Right then, a lady passenger said to me in her native French, "Ou est la toilette?" I couldn't believe it! And the Galley French Speaker burst out laughing! I proudly said, "La toilette est al'arriere." She said, in her high pitched French falsesetta, "Merci." The Galley and I laughed for a minute, but I needed to get out there to help with boarding.

Then, in Business Class a passenger showed me his boarding pass. He didn't speak English and wanted to know where his seat was. His ticket read 36F. I showed him where the seat numbers were located on the overhead bin, pointed to the back of the airplane and said, "al'arriere." I had learned the right phrases to use on the airplane.

Shopping was such fun in Paris, and we found copper pots. We found a store that sold copper pots, not just fondue pots, but sauce pans and skillets. Everything a French chef could want or need and they made wonderful gifts, from Paris! But oh, were they heavy to haul back home on the airplane. So, we enlisted the Pilots to help carry them for us. The next trip, the Pilots accompanied us to the copper pot store to buy gifts for their wives, they were so excited. Then we helped carry their copper pots home on the airplane.

Bill was my passenger on several trips to Paris and there was so much to share. We walked for an hour or two then enjoyed dinner at a favorite spot, "Cote Seine," along the river. We always had onion soup and escargot, then my favorite main course was salmon with a beurre blanc sauce.

On two separate occasions, I ventured out of the city to Giverny, the home and gardens of Monet. One time with Flight Attendants on a trip. We didn't nap at the hotel, we napped on the bus ride to Monet's home. The other time was with Bill on a vacation in France.

The tour of Giverny was exciting and informative. The gardens were like walking through Monet's paintings. I felt like I was his guest and he wanted to share his garden with me.

I Took This Picture Myself

Japan

The training for our new service to Japan began with three weeks of intensive focus at the Flight Academy and then weekends off. Most of the classroom work was cultural as we had already trained on the Boeing 747, however, this was a 747 SP which was a little smaller than our standard "74."

Every day we had an hour of Japanese language class, mostly greetings and numbers, telling time, and some basics like words for tea (ocha) and orange juice (orenji jusu). Saying "thank you" (arigato) was unusual as men could say "arigato" but women had to say "domo arigato," thank you very much, men didn't have to say "very much" every time. The cultural details made our training interesting and important.

First, we learned that the Japanese will not complain. They won't ask questions and they won't ask for anything. We wouldn't know if they liked the flight until six weeks to a month later and only the passenger loads would indicate whether the trip was a success. And, it was, as the loads continued to increase and we had more and more Japanese passengers on board.

That was an honor.

Honor is a focus of the Japanese. They also only want the best or finest brand or product. If a Japanese person chooses your product or uses your business, consider yourself successful. This was a big reason

American Airlines wanted this trip to be the best service and airline as perceived by and chosen by the Japanese.

As we learned in training, the Japanese won't ask for anything; they will accept something you offer so you have to anticipate what they might want. We often walked through the coach cabin with a tray of orange juice or water just to see if someone wanted anything. In First Class and Business Class we presented things constantly, so that didn't change.

When there were several Japanese passengers traveling together, it was easy to tell who the leader or ranking person was in the group as the others deferred to him. They let him speak first or choose first or go first. The rest of the group ordered the same thing whether they wanted it or not. We honored the order of their group.

One challenge that we learned in training: when the Japanese passenger nods his head up and down, it doesn't mean "yes." It means he heard you, and it may take some time and asking several questions before you can figure out what he wants or the answer to your question.

If Japanese people are "judging" you, they look at your shoes, they look at each other's shoes. I'm still not sure what they are trying to determine: your station in life (class), wealth, education? Whether you are on a city bus or an airplane, they check out your shoes.

We learned about the fine art of chopsticks: you don't place the chopsticks along the side of a fork, place the chopsticks in front of the plate, and use the "chopstick rest" or make one with the chopsticks' paper sleeve.

The flying time was very long so an additional service was added, a snack service. This was another learning experience: a Bento Box or Soba Noodles. A Bento Box contained small portions of rice, sushi, fish, or meat with another small vegetable mixture. The Soba Noodles were served hot or cold, sometimes with a broth or with toppings like scallions or vegetables. These were very tasty additions to our international service.

We also learned that in Japan it is permissible to slurp or make noise when you eat. Another difference in their culture is that the Japanese approve of taking bites off the fork or chopsticks. We cut a piece of (steak) just big enough for one bite then prepare another bite. They hold a bigger chunk of something and take several bites from it. This is not important, but it is interesting and unique enough for it to be included in our training.

Before our Japanese class graduation, we enjoyed dinner in a Japanese restaurant to practice using chopsticks and to see firsthand a briefing of Japanese food and customs. American had asked the restaurant to present a formal Japanese Tea Ceremony for our class to observe and partake. We were not going to have a Tea Ceremony on board for our passengers, but our training would not be complete without knowing about a Tea Ceremony. The Tea Ceremony is a ritual with precise details in an order that ends with the presentation of the cup of tea that is exact: the host gives the cup with one hand around the cup and the other hand under the cup. The guest receives the cup with two hands and a little bow of the head.

American had never tried a "dry run" before in order to practice or insure that all pieces of a service were in place and ready. On the 747 SP, on the ground, a week before our first flight to Japan, flight service and catering worked the new service from start to finish, in all three cabins (First Class, Business, and Coach). This tells you how important this trip was and how different the service was. Those of us that were scheduled to work the trip during the first week, were asked to attend/work this "dry run." And we were anxious to be included as we wanted to practice.

On my first trip to Japan, I was Purser. Everything was perfect and the flight wasn't full, which took some pressure off all of us. It still took a long time to serve, and, in fact we didn't feed the Cockpit crew for hours. There is a learning experience here: If it is a new service, the Cockpit should bring something to eat from home to give them patience. Our guys were great and didn't complain.

We stayed at a beautiful hotel near the Tokyo Airport in Narita, a little town nearby. The Cockpit crew was wide-eyed and immediately realized they were totally lost and had no control as their only training had been on the 747 SP. With no training or briefing on Japan or its culture, they didn't want us out of their sight!

We all planned to meet in the lobby of the hotel at 3:00 in the afternoon and took a van provided by the hotel into Narita. The first stop in Narita was at none other than "McDonald's!" The Cockpit crew lit up. We all enjoyed McDonald's on that first trip but we Flight Attendants did venture out to look around and marvel at this new destination and culture.

The main street looked like an open-air market. Some stores sold clothes or shoes, but one store sold live eels! And another: eel-skin wallets and eel-skin eye glass cases. Several of us found a restaurant to have tea and enjoyed the table and chairs so close to the ground.

The flying time from Dallas to Tokyo was a long 12 hours. If a stronger head-wind developed and the flying time increased closer to 13 hours, the flight had to stop for fuel. This didn't happen very often but Seattle or Anchorage were the two likely airports prepared for this quick fill-up. It needed to be quick as the long duty-day for the Flight Attendants and Cockpit crew couldn't be extended. If the fueling took too long it would mean that the trip had to spend the night in Seattle or Anchorage, inconveniencing everyone. This didn't happen very often. I never had to stop for fuel.

We learned by looking around in Narita that nothing was written in English. In all our other foreign destinations, English was written somewhere to explain a sign or information about items in a museum or food, or directions. But in Narita, no English.

So, it was a big surprise after a couple of trips to see a "sandwich board" advertisement in English on the street across from McDonald's. It invited tourists to "Take a chance, take Japanese with a Japanese tutor!" I thought, if I am going to fly this trip for a year or so, I could learn Japanese and maybe to read it, write it? Several of us tried it!

We discovered that our tutor was from Narita but graduated from Ethan, a small University in Indiana. He worked his way through college tutoring students taking Japanese.

The difficult part is that he started our studies with Japanese grammar. I wanted to learn to say something. And, he had a lisp.

At the end of the first class, he stood at the door to say goodbye, I bowed and said, how do you say: "How much is it?" It was only then that I realized that I could only count to ten. I had to write down and practice his answer and work on my numbers.

The classes were difficult but interesting and I did come away with some words and phrases. But only four classes into our studies, our teacher informed us that JAL (Japanese Airlines) had hired him to teach their mechanics English and he no longer could teach our class.

We had taken a chance.

Flying to Japan was wonderful. I flew to Japan exclusively for almost two years, 1987-1989.

I resumed flying to Europe when we added Madrid and Brussels out of Dallas. Then I was able to hold American Airlines' inaugural flight to Sydney, Australia on the MD-11.

On The List

As we were preparing for our trip from Dallas to Frankfurt, the agent came on board to brief us that an elderly man was being sent back to Germany by our Customs and Immigration Department at DFW.

This man had arrived in Dallas that afternoon with his son and his son's wife and two grandchildren, to visit America for the first time. It was explained to us that the elderly man didn't speak English, only German, and he would be traveling back to Frankfurt alone.

I asked the agent if the man understood why he was being sent back to Germany? The agent said yes. I asked about who was going to meet him when we arrived? Was his baggage on board, did he have any medications with him? All these details had been taken care of.

The agent went back out to the gate to bring the passenger on board, I quickly told the Captain and then we saw this quite elderly man stooped, with a cane, in a suit and tie coming down the jet bridge. He was accompanied by the agent, his son, and a police officer. I shook hands with the son, then asked again who would be meeting his father in Frankfurt? Then I explained to his son that an agent would take him through customs and immigration in Germany.

They said their good-byes and I took the elderly man to his seat in Business Class where he would sit alone and we could watch him the whole flight.

He didn't eat or read, he just sat looking straight ahead. Our Business Class Flight Attendant German Speaker asked him about something to eat or drink and he said no.

This man had been in charge of a concentration camp during World War II and his name was on a list of Germans not allowed in the United States.

The agent that met our flight knew all about this man and who was supposed to meet him in baggage claim.

I didn't write the man's name down to report here but it was a very unusual circumstance and interesting to know that "The List" is still on watch.

The Gulf War

When Iraq invaded Kuwait in 1991 our country responded. Immediately things changed on our trips with new security in place. I was Purser on this trip, flying from Dallas to Frankfurt, Germany.

The first change that surprised us was that the Captain had to board the airplane early while the co-pilot remained in operations to file the flight plan. The Captain stood at the front door of the plane before any of us boarded in order for him to check each of our American Airlines I.D. badges as we stepped on the plane. After all our Flight Attendants were on board and had put our suitcases away, the Captain called us to First Class for a briefing.

During the briefing, he gave us information about our arrival in Frankfurt and that American Airlines had changed our hotel. We had been staying in Mainz, now we were going to be staying at the hotel next to the airport terminal building. The Captain said when we received our room keys he wanted a list of our names and room numbers in case we had to leave for some reason in a hurry, even in the middle of the night. He said we might have to knock on doors in order to not use the phones.

This was all very alarming. He said that we might be stuck away from home for an extended amount of time. Several of us, including the Captain and Co-Pilot, whose fathers had been in World War II brought extra money in case we were detained. My Dad was a pilot in WW II and the captain on his airplanes. Dad told our family about an occasion when his crew was detained in Africa. He had a gun under his pillow and a large sum of money in case he had to buy his crew out of that situation. He was with the Fourth Ferrying Group based in Memphis and then Fireball Express based in Miami.

The scariest thing in our situation was after the passengers deplaned in Frankfurt, German Airport Security came onto our airplane to brief us and escort us (the crew) off the airplane. The briefing was to explain our walk through the airport and over to the hotel. Our thirteen crew members were instructed to walk in a single line (not bunched together). The armed security guards would be at the front and back of the line and at intervals along the line. We were also aware of Security Guards, with guns, watching us from balconies in the airport.

When we arrived at the hotel, our crew was taken straight to a conference room. Security at the hotel didn't want us waiting in the lobby. I went to the front desk with the Captain, gave the clerk our list of names, then we went to the conference room to await our room keys.

Even in other cities in Europe, we didn't go into town, but stayed at the closest hotel to the airport. On every trip the Captain checked our I.D. as we boarded the airplane and gave us a briefing before the passengers boarded.

These procedures stopped when the crises ended in Kuwait and Iraq.

When the Saints Go Marching In

There are a couple of stories on the airplane about St. Andrews Presbyterian College that really make me shake my head in amazement.

I was so excited to arrive in Laurinburg, North Carolina and become a college girl. This was the perfect school for me as it was small, co-ed, four year, with a business, liberal arts, and sciences focus. Now they have added an incredible Equine Science major. It also has an award-winning Bagpipe Band.

It had co-ed dorms. You had to earn the privilege to live in a co-ed dorm, through good grades, honor, and responsibility. The co-ed dorms were not co-ed rooms and they were not for freshmen.

St. Andrews introduced co-ed physical education with an attitude that men and women need to learn how to play together. High school and college separate men and women's teams, no matter what sport. Golf is a sport that college men and women can learn and enjoy together.

My interest was in child psychology; as a result, I was studying to be a kindergarten or elementary school teacher.

I had the perfect roommate from Georgia and wonderful suitemates who are my close friends to this day. We try to get together every Fall. In fact, I still send alumni donations and attend reunions. I love that school, now it has qualified for and become St. Andrews University.

Here is a non-airplane, college-freshman-story that makes me laugh.

We, as a group, decided we were going to smoke. We gathered in one room of our suite and somebody had a pack of cigarettes and some matches. We passed out the cigarettes, I think there were five of us and we lit up together.

I didn't know you had to inhale, I was mostly looking at my hand with a cigarette in it. My Mother smoked, a lot, she had beautiful hands, and she looked so glamorous smoking, so the first thing I did was look in the mirror to see if I looked glamorous too. I looked like I was playing dress-up. I put the cigarette out and never smoked again. It wasn't me.

St. Andrews was one of the first colleges to be built to accommodate disabled students in dorms, classrooms, and all facilities.

They had notable basketball and soccer teams and this Fall St. Andrews will have their first football game in their new stadium. Which brings me to the fact that St. Andrews' fight song still is, "When the Saints Go Marching In!"

During spring break of my freshman year at St. Andrews, I was at home in Alexandria and needed to see if I could find a job for the summer months. Before I started my search, Reva, a friend of mine from high school, in fact, my best friend from high school, called to ask me if I had gotten a job for the summer. She was a freshman at Maryville College in Tennessee. I said no, had she?

She said that her Dad was waiting until we got home to see if any of us wanted to work in the summer. He already had a job for us, four of us who were high school friends, now college girls. The job was in New York City at the 1964 World's Fair! He had also contracted for an apartment for us. All four of us accepted the job.

Reva's father was a lawyer in D.C. who had partnered with three other lawyers (one from Texas) to establish and underwrite the "African Pavilion" at the New York World's Fair. These lawyers brought together the four of us and two college students from Texas. There were also Africans employed who spoke excellent English and who could explain some of the displays that were presented.

We American college students rotated in positions as cashiers, ticket-takers, host and hostesses, and pages (ran errands). Our apartment was small, in Queens, but adequate for us. The building mostly housed students working at the World's Fair and sometimes in the evening the building was like a big open house dorm.

In the middle of June, we had been working at the World's Fair for about a month, I received a letter from St. Andrews that my Mother had forwarded to me. The letter said I had to attend summer school in order to continue at St. Andrews. I guessed because of my grades. I didn't have a guidance counselor so I couldn't ask her.

I was devastated, first of all, that summer school had already started. Now, I had a dream-come-true job in New York City, I couldn't just leave, I was trained and the African Pavilion would be shorthanded if I left.

I worked at the World's Fair all summer, thinking the whole time about not being a sophomore in college or being with my friends at St. Andrews. What was I going to do now? What about being a teacher?

I'll go to summer school next summer…but I want to fly.

OK, now fast forward, or maybe slow forward twenty-two years.

I was married, lived in California, commuted to Dallas, flew international, I was the Purser on these long-haul flights, I spoke some Spanish, German, French, and a little (very little) Japanese, I loved my job and I was content.

On this Hawaii trip our layover was at the Ala Moana Hotel and now our crew arrived at the gate for our DC-10 flight back to Dallas. I was working as Purser. The gate area was busy and a line had formed with passengers in wheelchairs ready to be pre-boarded. The passengers in wheel chairs seemed to be in a group, college age, maybe ten of them. The gate agent boarded with us to say we needed to start boarding the wheelchair passengers right away as it would take a while and then the wheelchairs had to be put in cargo.

I went out with the agent to meet the leaders of this group and, funny, I recognized the man in charge.

Oh, my gosh, it was Rodger Decker, Dean of Admissions from St. Andrews! Everyone liked him, including me.

Now, I meet him in Honolulu as Purser in charge of getting his 10 disabled students to Dallas so that they can connect to Raleigh-Durham, North Carolina.

Some of the students could move around a little so they didn't all have to be seated on the aisle. They were really glad to meet me and we could talk about St. Andrews; I loved meeting them. The Flight Attendants were wonderful to them and the whole experience was amazing. It gave me closure. I had a nice talk with Dean Decker, he remembered me and my situation from long ago and we agreed that: **The Lord works in Wondrous Ways.**

Here is another airplane story on the 747 from Dallas to Honolulu and that's a l-o-n-g flight, close to seven hours long. I was sitting on my jumpseat in coach (I wasn't Purser on this trip) for taxi-away and take-off when I spoke to some young guys across from my jump seat who were traveling together. I asked them about their trip to Hawaii and one said he had just graduated from college the day before and his parents had given him this trip to Hawaii as a graduation gift; his friend's parents did the same.

I asked him what school? He said, "Saint Andrews, a small college in North Carolina, you probably have never heard of it." I almost fell off the jumpseat! I said, "I went there, in Laurinburg, right?" He was shocked! and said, "When I was sitting there yesterday, waiting for my name to be called, I thought, 'I am never going to meet anyone who has heard of this little college, no matter where I go.' And, here you are the next day."

Of course, I wanted a college education. As I started flying I considered myself a college girl with a brief interruption while fulfilling my dream of being a stewardess.

After flying for three years I decided to settle down with this job. The work was meaty and meaningful.

Traveling all over the country, then flying international was like earning a master's degree in psychology. The emergency and medical training that was such a big part of our job equaled having one EMT (Emergency Medical Technician) for every fifty passengers on the airplane.

Who would have guessed that I would fly for 37 years?

Bill's Boys

Sean Thomas McNeice came to live with us in Mission Viejo at the start of his freshman year in high school. He had been living with his mother and younger brother, Darrin in Pennsylvania.

I probably had the bigger adjustment as I was now a "mom" with new responsibilities and cooking duties, and, he was about seven inches taller than me. It was wonderful for Bill to have Sean with him while I was away on trips. They had "bonding" time and "M.A.S.H." to share on TV.

I'll cut lots of stories short and just tell you about Sean's accomplishments. Mission Viejo High School started a new program just as Sean was starting his sophomore year. It was the Junior Reserve Officer Training Corps (JROTC) and he joined with our permission. He did so well that during his senior year in high school he was the Commander of his JROTC unit.

When Sean was 17 years old, still in high School, he joined the U.S. Army Reserve, again with our permission. His basic training was in South Carolina, and he came home skinny and proud.

Sean's Army Reserve unit was based in Camp Pendleton, California, which is a Marine base, but Sean's Army unit was on Larks. Larks are Army amphibious machines that take Marines and their equipment from shore to ships out in the ocean.

Not long after joining the Army Reserve, Sean's Lark was training out in the Pacific when a dangerous wave pushed a soldier overboard, it broke his arm, leg, and he lost some teeth. Sean didn't check with anyone, he just jumped into the water and saved him. Sean received a medal for saving the soldier.

After high school, Sean attended a junior college. He was living at home and started dropping his classes. Then, one day, he received a letter from the California Maritime Academy in Vallejo, California, saying that he had been accepted as a student the next year. Sean had sent a letter to CMA stating he wanted to go to the Academy and gave them his history. It was a letter, not an application form. Bill and I didn't know anything about it! The California Maritime Academy required Chemistry and SAT tests, but Sean didn't have either! The letter they sent said they were accepting him because of his military aptitude.

Sean graduated in four years. Upon graduation in 1989, from CMA, Sean's rank was "Third Mate" on cargo ships. Training cruises over the summer months had given him lots of practice in the duties of the officers on board different types of cargo ships including: oil tankers, bulk cargo (coal, fertilizer), containers, and cars.

He sailed all over the world, mostly on container ships that were three football fields long. Sean retired as a Captain from going out to sea four or five months at a time and today he is Associate Professor for Texas A&M Maritime Academy. He teaches Bridge Resource Management on simulators in Galveston.

Sean still maintains his home in Texas, living close to his two daughters.

DARRIN MCNEICE

Darrin McNeice, Bill's younger son, has a good story too.

Darrin graduated from the University of West Virginia with a major in Biology. He was disappointed with his first job at a fish farm in Vancouver, British Columbia. We don't know if it was the people or the fish, but it wasn't for him.

Bill and Darrin wrote each other often and Darrin told us he was having a difficult time finding another job, so he worked part time at L.L. Bean, still out in Vancouver. In one letter back to Darrin, Bill mentioned that American Airlines had cancelled their nepotism policy. It was just one sentence in a long letter.

Maybe Darrin looked it up, but with no conversation, two months later he called us and said, "I have an interview with American tomorrow, is there anything I should know?"

Bill and I went to his graduation from "Stew School" in 1991, at the American Airlines Training School in Ft. Worth, Texas. Oh, what a beautiful class they were, highly educated with men and women ready to "Fly High."

The class sang "Wind Beneath My Wings" to the audience of parents and friends.

I'm going to take a moment here to say that the training had changed from the "flash mob songs" to more of a finishing school, like learning how to set a table and learning to be a wine expert. Not as much focus on mascara and nail polish, but instead on how to conceal sweating and more of a "silent service," rather than "Chatty Cathy." Certainly cheerful, but not cheerleader. Smiling, but not in your face. Demure.

Although not required, most of our Flight Attendants have degrees now. I flew with a Flight Attendant with a D.M.D. in Dentistry. Her Dad wanted her to be a dentist, but she wanted to fly. She was senior to me and she was still flying when I retired.

There was a group of guys based in Dallas who were working their way through medical school flying with American Airlines. By the time they had earned their medical degrees, they had good seniority and were flying all over the world. Beside the fact that they were earning good money, they didn't want to stop flying. So, they opened a medical clinic and staffed the Doctors according to their flying schedule each month.

The Vietnam Vets that started flying with us when the war was over are probably retired from American by now.

Darrin started his flying years out of New York City. With his class, he immediately trained for "over-water" in order to qualify for international trips right away. He spoke some French, which helped as well.

No one put him in the overhead rack on his first trip.

But, like I did, he had several roommates to start out, except it was three girls and two guys. Times have changed.

In February 1992, about a year after he started flying, he was "dead-heading," which means he was going from one city to another, on duty, in uniform, but not working the trip. He was assigned a First Class seat. The Flight Attendant working First Class, Jaimie, was a beautiful blond and when she needed something in the overhead bin, Darrin jumped up to get it for her. Later they talked for a few minutes and he found out it was her second flight out of Stew School. Jaimie was from Dallas and had graduated from North Texas University with a major in Political Science, but she wanted to fly.

In August that same year, 1992, Darrin and Jaimie were married, in New York, without any family members present. Then Bill and I had a wonderful reception for them at our house in Mission Viejo. The bride and groom were beautiful and glowing. They stood with me at the front door to meet our friends and neighbors, like a receiving line. Bill stood farther into the foyer to direct our guests to the bar. Sean was there and some of my Flight Attendant friends and their husbands also came to the party. After a light meal and cutting the wedding cake, we all assembled in the living room for Jaimie and Darrin to open presents. Well, (ooo, I just got chills), when Jaimie, then Darrin, read the card from each present, they looked up around the room, found the person/couple who gave them that gift to thank them. They had paid attention meeting every friend and what their names were and could pick him or her out of the crowd in that short time. There may have been 25 people there. Did I say that they still give name association class in Stew School? But, in our living room, that bride and groom were gifted in remembering names. We were so proud of them and many of our friends were astounded at the personal attention.

In 1996 on a trip to Paris, I was scheduled to be the Purser, and Jaimie was scheduled to be the "Business Class Galley" (work the galley position on the Boeing 767). Darrin traded trips to be the "First Class Galley," and all of a sudden we were all on the same flight and became "The Flying McNeices!" Well, Bill couldn't miss this so he came with us as our passenger in First Class.

Bill took us to dinner at Cote Seine our favorite place along the river. The whole trip worked out perfectly. Bill was in Business Class for the trip back to Dallas as First Class was full. It is such a beautiful memory.

Darrin started working for American's Flight Attendant Union. He helped to set up the Union's computer connections just as computers were coming on-line. He was so good he became the Union's "computer guru."

A few years later, Darrin was offered a job in sales with a metals distributor in California. So he took an "early out" package with American.

He flew with American Airlines for ten years based in New York, Miami, and Dallas. Today he is working in California. His beautiful wife, Jaimie is based in San Francisco and they have a brilliant son, James, who is fourteen.

I'm so proud of Bill's Boys.

Sean Back from Army Boot Camp in South Carolina, 17 years old

Sean's Graduation California Maritime Academy, 1989

Darrin and Jaimie's Reception 1992

Tina, Darrin, Jaimie, and Bill McNeice
Bill couldn't miss this trip to Paris, 1996

Have You Ever Been Scared?

The other day one of my tennis friends asked me, "Have you ever been scared while working on the airplane?"

With just a moment's thought I said, "No, because of our incredible training." Our training covers just about everything we need on the airplane. When an emergency occurs, we don't stand around thinking, "What should I do?" We have practiced and talked about circumstances and "What ifs" so often that "We are ready."

Having said that ....

On a trip from Dallas to Frankfurt, our dinner service in the cabin was complete. I went to the cockpit to ask them about their entree choice for dinner. As usual, I didn't say anything until I could see they weren't busy.

The Captain said to the Flight Engineer, "Now what is it?" The Flight Engineer said a number.

Then the Captain said to me, "What's for dinner?" I gave them the choices and served the Co-Pilot and Engineer first. In a little while I went up to serve the Captain's dinner, he was saying to the Engineer, "Now what is it?" And the Captain turned around in his seat to look at a dial on the Engineer's panel of instruments behind the Co-Pilot's seat. As I served the tray to the Captain he said (to the Engineer): "Tell me if it goes down to (a number)."

In a few minutes, I went up to get the trays and now I wanted to know "What's up?" The atmosphere in the Cockpit seemed a little different. The trays were piled on the extra jumpseat. I could see that the Captain hadn't eaten and he was on the radio; the Engineer was at full alert facing his instrument panel.

The Captain to the Engineer: "Now what is it?" With the Engineer's answer, he said to me, "Tina, our hydraulic fluid is going down and it looks like we are going to have to divert to Gander, Newfoundland."

I asked him, "Do we need to prepare for an emergency landing?" He said, "No, as long as we can get the landing gear down, the hydraulic fluid is still okay for now, but not to land in Frankfurt." He said, "We will probably have to spend the night in Gander as I don't know when American can get a new airplane to us, and they need to bring a couple of mechanics to fix this problem."

We landed just fine, but then we had to wait on the airplane for two hours without any explanation. We found out that the ground personnel were trying to find places for us (all of us) to stay. Finally, we were able to deplane into the terminal building that had one big waiting area.

While we sat in the terminal a passenger, in tears, got my attention. She said she was going to her father's funeral the next day in Germany. "How long will this take? When will we get there?"

Another man got my attention saying stitches in his leg had come apart and he was bleeding, could he get some help? He knew that altitude in flight makes some people's skin swell and you're not supposed to fly with stitches, but he thought he would be fine. We found some ice.

Another lady had an infant and a two-year old.

You get the point, this was difficult for everyone. There, in the terminal, we gave emotional first-aid.

The ground personnel were wonderful. They found a motel near the airport for our crew and a few passengers, then they found some homes that welcomed our passengers until an airplane came the next day.

The airplane brought mechanics for our airplane, and just picked up our passengers and their baggage and took them to Frankfurt. We stayed in Gander two nights until our plane was repaired enough to fly back to Dallas with no passengers.

Note: The people in Gander are wonderful. When our "9/11 crisis" closed American Air Space, Gander and other communities in Canada "took in" airline passengers for ten days. They are truly good neighbors.

Miami

Senior in Miami

Several of us who were based in Dallas transferred to Miami without consulting each other. The common thread is that we married older men and these older men retired when we still had about ten years to go to qualify for full retirement at age 55. Living in south Florida was like retiring to a resort; we were retired on our days off.

Surprised to see each other in Miami's operations, we found out that we didn't live in Miami, we lived across the state of Florida in Ft. Myers, Bonita Springs, and Naples. We all flew international and we were all on different trips: to London, Frankfurt, Madrid, and Paris and these trips all left Miami (MIA) about the same time in the evening to arrive in Europe in mid-morning.

New to Southwest Florida, we helped each other find a dentist, "lady-business" doctor, grocery store, beauty salon, etc. We tried to commute together on stand-by out of the Ft. Myer's airport or out of Naples but that became too stressful, if we didn't get on the flight we had to jump in the car and drive two hours and 40 minutes to Miami. We tried to drive together, but that wasn't smooth either.

We drove by ourselves. The employee parking lot was not far from where my Dad had been based during WWII.

Commuting across the Everglades on Alligator Alley (Route 75) from Bonita Springs and Naples to the Miami Airport for nine years was a marvel. The Everglades gave endless sights and events to enjoy every trip with the exotic birds, clouds, and storms as well as the wild-fires, and even some alligators. The great stands of trees: Cypress, Slash Pines, Mangroves, Gumbo Limbo, Southern Live Oaks, and differ-ent kinds of Palms, the sawgrass marshes, wildflowers, saw palmettos, ferns, and sugar cane all flourish in the Everglades. The Federal Gov-ernment designated two areas as National Parks, Big Cypress National Park in the Southwest and Everglades National Park closer to Miami.

UNESCO (United Nations Educational Scientific and Cultural Organization) listed the Everglades as a Heritage Site, Cultural and Natural.

I discovered a fascinating detail driving home from Paris and Ma-drid: after boarding the passengers in Europe, leaving the gate, take-off, flying across the Atlantic, deplaning the passengers in Miami, going through customs, turning in the money (duty free) and reports, taking the bus to the employee parking lot, driving across Alligator Alley at a constant speed: (cruise control, 72 mph).

I listened to the radio most of the way across Alligator Alley, then heard the radio announcer, Al Baxa, on WAVV 101.1 FM sign off his shift at 6:45 pm at the same intersection in Bonita Springs every trip!

The longer I drove over to work, the commute was getting to me and my pals, the extra half hour to drive to the employee parking lot and take the bus to operations in the terminal building was getting old.

We, who were getting ready to retire, didn't talk about our decisions to not park in the employee parking lot any more. We parked in the public parking garage at the terminal building and paid full fare, no discounts. It was very extravagant, we called it "princess parking." It was a lot faster and if we timed it right and our flight was as "on time" as usual, we didn't have to pay for an extra day.

One time in Madrid, while we were boarding, the Captain came out of the cockpit and said, "Get these people on here, let's get going, I 'princess parked!'"

Madrid had its special details. First of all, they ate late!! We as a crew and as Americans wanted the evening to start, maybe with a drink, about 6:00 or at the latest, 7:00 pm. In Madrid, they started at 9:00! We found very few places that opened at 7:00 or 8:00. They opened later because they took a nap or rested in the afternoon. It was cultural. We adjusted.

The atmosphere of the places that we found to have dinner seemed rather formal. In fact, Madrid is very formal. Our crew enjoyed dinner together when we shared a big skillet of Paella which included shrimp, fish, chicken, and rice. Then during the summer the Spanish served Gazpacho (cold tomato and cucumber soup) as a specialty as well as Manchego Cheese.

Soccer season wrapped you into the festivities just walking down the street! Taverns, pubs, bars boiled over with noise and laughter and fun, cheering for whoever played that night, but Oh! My! when Spanish teams played, it was off the charts!

Some of us became followers of Flamenco Dancing as we found dinner shows, or "Tablao" where Flamenco Shows performed all evening. We learned that the Spanish taught Flamenco Dancing in school as a physical education class for boys and girls. During dinner one evening the Flamenco Dancers, a man and woman, began their beautiful presentation, then they pulled from the audience a boy and girl, teenagers, not in any costume, and they danced like professionals.

I could hold the Purser position to Madrid with four day weekends off every month out of Miami, I loved it!

Danya Archbold & Tina in Madrid
August 2001, just before September 11th attack on New York city

Madrid to Miami

This trip is easy to remember as first of all it was an "event," second, I saved several reports that contain details of just what happened.

Flight 69, October 31, 1996, Madrid to Miami, on a Boeing 767, the service went smoothly for our full load of passengers in all cabins. But sometime during the movie, the coach Flight Attendants became aware of a passenger standing up in the back near the aft galley. I say "became aware" as people stand up and sit down and maybe stand up for a while, maybe visit with another passenger … this man had several drinks, but he just stood there, in the way of others moving around. The coach Flight Attendants asked him to sit down, he didn't.

The coach F/As were taking turns going on their breaks, the F/A working as the coach galley went on his break and as he left the galley he said to the standing passenger "Go sit down!"

Every once in a while, he went into the lavatory and it seemed like he was becoming agitated, even drunk. At one point a Flight Attendant checked the lavatory after he came out, it was covered in urine and they had to lock off that lav. The coach Spanish Speaker told him in Spanish to sit down, he understood English and Spanish, but he didn't sit down.

I was working as Purser on this trip and received a call from a coach Flight Attendant asking me to come back to speak to this passenger and tell him to sit down and get out of the way. I did, he didn't move.

I went up to the cockpit to tell the Captain about our problem passenger and the Captain stood up and said, "I'll talk to him." On the way out of the cockpit the Captain said, "Should I wear my hat? How tall is he?" I said, "wear your hat."

The Captain was tall and handsome and probably a former Marine, we were so proud when he came back to save the day.

When the Captain walked through the cabin and approached the passenger. He said (not in a "good ole boy" way, but not confrontational)

"I understand that the F/As have asked you to sit down and you ..." the bad guy pounded his finger into the Captain's chest and said something to him in Spanish. The Spanish speaking Flight Attendant backed up. I never found out what the bad guy said to the Captain in Spanish.

The Captain stood stoic, face to face, eye to eye, with this guy and said, "I suggest you ..." The guy knocked the Captain's hat off. The Captain turned around with a military "about face" and returned to the cockpit. The Spanish speaking F/A quickly picked up his hat and took it to the cockpit.

Note: either of those two things the passenger did would qualify to put him in jail.

About this time the coach galley F/A returned from his break and said "That guy is still standing there!" The other F/As told him about the Captain coming back to speak to the passenger.

I had returned to First Class as it was almost time to prepare our last service before landing in Miami, we try to start the service about an hour and a half out.

A coach Flight Attendant called me: "Get back here fast, the guy just came into the galley with his fist clinched ready to attack the galley F/A!"

I got there just in time, they were nose to nose—I pushed myself between them facing the bad guy and said to the galley, "You take my place in First Class (he was Purser qualified), I'll work galley back here," as he left I said, "and tell the Captain!"

During all this the lady passenger with her middle seat next to the bad guy, traded places with her husband in case the bad guy ever sat down.

With me standing there facing ... not exactly facing him, I'm short you know, it was terrible to have to look up at this bad guy, he left the galley and went back to stand in his spot.

I turned around and thought, hmmm, I haven't worked coach galley in a long time. I got the two liquor carts out for the aisle F/As to start setting up for the snack service, when, over the P.A. the Captain said, "Flight Attendants prepare for landing, we'll be landing in Bermuda in 20 minutes." You could feel the nose of the airplane headed down in a steep descent.

The guy sat down.

I started putting things away in the galley when the F/A who had been working coach galley came back and took over, I returned to First Class.

We were on the ground in no time and as we arrived at the gate (no jet bridge, we were in a remote area) there were six Constables (Policemen) standing at attention lined up in front of where the mobile steps were rolled up to the forward left door.

I made my "Prepare for arrival" P.A. for the Flight Attendants to detach the slides from the doors. An additional mobile staircase was attached to the aft left door. Two Constables came up the stairs from the front and four Constables from the back stairs. They must have known the bad guy's seat number and went right to his seat. He didn't put up any fight as they took him off through the aft door and down the stairs in handcuffs.

The Captain had gotten off the plane down the front stairs when the front door opened as he needed to talk to Bermuda's operations and American's dispatch in Miami and file a new flight plan.

While the Captain was off the plane I made a P.A. to explain to our passengers about the drunk passenger that wouldn't sit down and about how stoic and courageous our Captain was.

When the Captain came back on board, the passengers gave a big applause.

We were only on the ground a short time as we all knew many of our passengers had close connections in Miami.

During the service to MIA a passenger in First Class asked me how much you had to drink to get kicked off an airplane? Most of the passengers were subdued and quiet all the way to MIA. We dutifully passed out the customs forms and the passengers were attentive and cooperative.

The passengers didn't find out about the outcome of this event...

The man was from Honduras. He spent three days in jail in Bermuda and five months in jail or detention in Honduras.

September 11, 2001

September 11, 2001, a day that changed us all. I was on vacation for the month of September. Bill was playing tennis and I had left home to go to the tennis courts, but forgot something. So I went back home, ran inside to get it, left the car running, but there was a beep that I had a message on the phone.

I stopped real quick to hear the message, I recognized the voice and he said, "I am sure glad Stan retired last year, this is going to be bad." And he hung up. What? It was Carl Larson from our church. What did he mean?

I ran in and turned on the TV, and there it was — the Trade Center Tower was on fire. What was this? In that moment while I was watching, the second airplane circled a little and slammed into the second Tower!

I didn't cry, I paced the floor. At some point, I went out and turned off the car. The Pentagon, the field in Pennsylvania, as you know, it went on and on.

Bill got the news and came home. I didn't sit down all day.

That was Tuesday, on Thursday Bill and I had a pot-luck dinner for all of my Flight Attendant friends in our area. We needed to hug each other, we needed to cry, we had to mentally get ready to go back to work. Our husbands stood close together with a drink and talked. We were in the kitchen and kept hugging, after a while we calmed down, being together helped. I turned on some music, we ate and started thinking again. One of our pals was stuck in Paris.

I had flown with one of the Flight Attendants that was on the airplane that went into the Pentagon. That crew was based in Washington, D.C. Another interesting detail is that two of the Flight Attendants on that flight were husband and wife, from Culpeper, Virginia. They were named Jennifer and Kenneth. They flew together so often that Flight Attendants in Washington called them Kenifer. As in, "I'm flying with Kenifer." Culpeper has built a memorial in a park in their honor.

My first trip back to work was to Paris, October 1st. The passengers were on alert, wide eyed, and jumpy when we walked by. They didn't relax until November and didn't sleep through the night until December.

We Flight Attendants noticed that during boarding some men looked at each other and gave a slight nod (like: we can depend on each other). Interesting. And, some men asked for an aisle seat rather than a window seat in First Class to be ready if needed, they even gave us a slight nod.

We Flight Attendants didn't have any weapons or protection and felt vulnerable yet protective of our Pilots and cockpit. "On the fly" we came up with all we had. A pot of hot coffee! If someone threatened us, throw hot coffee on them, it may not kill them, but it might slow them down, then some passengers could help. Another innovation was to bring out the carts, arrange the carts in front of the cockpit door at different angles, which would again slow them down and then after throwing hot coffee on them, the passengers could help subdue them.

No one has ever recognized and thanked the person who made the brilliant decision to close the American air space on September 11, 2001. That decision may have stopped more hijackings. We will forever honor that person.

After I wrote about not knowing who made the decision of closing

American air space during/after the attacks and hijackings on September 11th, I did some research.

I Googled, "Who made the decision to close American Air Space on September 11, 2001?"

The answer is the FAA. There may not have been a single person as I found out that first there was a "ground stop," which means that all take-offs and landings were suspended in New York. Then the New York air space was closed, then the Washington, D.C. air space was closed...then all American air space was closed.

After the national trauma of 9/11, we Flight Attendants were issued handcuffs in a blue pouch. With the help of the volunteer and alert passengers, we were ready to handle a passenger that had to be subdued.

That's still not a weapon but we could keep a "bad guy" contained without having to wrestle with him the whole time until the airplane landed.

The Lady in Black

It was plain to see at age four (busy year) that I was pigeon-toed. My Pediatrician in Arlington, Virginia, Dr. Dorothy Whipple, didn't want to put me into a brace to straighten me out so she recommended that I start ballet right away. My Mother called around and asked about a local ballet teacher and discovered Heidi Pope, from Austria, teaching in Fairlington which was near where we lived. We found her studio and Mother asked if I could join her class of younger students. Heidi said that she didn't accept four year olds, maybe I could start when I was five. But, being as we were there, we could watch, then she said I could stand at the back of the class.

Mother had already gotten me ballet shoes, they were black and I had very casual clothes on, so I stood in the back of the class of maybe eight little girls. I did everything they did. I watched the teacher, she was easy to follow. We went through first foot position, on through fifth position. We moved our arms with the different foot positions. Then she added plies. She reviewed how to hold our hands. It was all new to me, but I loved it.

At the end of that class, Heidi Pope accepted me as a student, I took ballet from her for six years before we moved to Houston. It was so fulfilling, it was me. Although her style was not classical ballet, I later figured out that it was more modern dance. We did work on parts of

Swan Lake and the Nutcracker and we actually performed "Peter and the Wolf" one year in front of an audience for our recital.

When I was in the second grade, we moved to Alexandria, not far away and Heidi had a ballet studio near our new house in Hollin Hall.

Heidi Pope made sure we knew how to waltz and rumba and we learned other dances that would be considered ballroom dancing today, but she also encouraged us in another direction: choreography. She designed a dance that we were to follow and practice, then she would design a different dance and we practiced that. She said for us to pick out a song we liked and design a dance ourselves, then perform it for our class. I chose Frank Sinatra's "Young at Heart." It was fun practicing in our family's living room, I was nine.

I took ballet on and off through our moves to Houston and Ft. Worth then back to Alexandria. In total I took ballet for fifteen years.

One constant in all this ballet, no matter where or what age, was what we wore, the leotard, the black leotard, sometimes short sleeves, sometimes long sleeves, with or without black leggings, and ballet shoes. When I was in the first grade, my favorite color was black. I had been taking ballet for two years, everyone else's favorite color was blue or pink. My favorite color is still black and I wear a lot of black. Finally, after all these years I am realizing that when I look at myself in the mirror, if I am wearing black, I look like myself.

Now that I am older and considered "Senior," I thank all those years of ballet for a very strong back and excellent balance which I used on the airplane every day for thirty-seven years.

I still take ballroom dance lessons.

If It's Not Boeing, I'm Not Going

I said that to make you laugh.

Our Kiwi Chapter has chanted those words many times.

Boeing bought McDonald Douglas in 1996, so our years of flying the DC-10 and MD-11 absorbed into our chant.

Boeing is an American company and most of the airplane parts are American made.

The Boeing simulators that we Flight Attendants train on and the Pilots train on at the Flight Academy in Ft. Worth are top of the line and have given us confidence in their airplanes, equipment, and innovations.

The Boeing 767 then 777 were assigned to fly to Europe and South America. After I transferred to Miami, I mostly flew the Boeing 767 to London, Paris, Frankfurt, and Madrid.

As American prepared to buy some Airbus airplanes, we took our Pilots to Paris to go through the Airbus pilot training in Toulouse, France.

I did qualify on the Airbus 320 but only worked it one month...

Because...If It's Not Boeing, I'm Not Going.

Long Black Socks

Tootie, one of my supervisors in Washington, D.C., was senior enough to stop working as a supervisor and trained for the Military Airlift Command (MAC) trips to Vietnam. She flew to Vietnam for several years. After Vietnam, she continued to fly out of D.C.

When the day came that she worked her last trip home into Washington, the Captain made a P.A. telling the passengers it was Tootie's last trip. The passengers gave her big applause and some shook her hand as they got off the airplane. Then, with the passengers off, the crew picked up their suitcases and as she walked off the plane she started singing, "One less bell to answer, one less egg to fry, one less man to pick up after, I should be happy . . ."

Retired American Airlines Flight Attendants are known as "Kiwis." We are "birds that don't fly." My Kiwi Chapter is in Ft. Myers, Florida, and I have friends in the Naples Chapter. We are a close-knit nest of birds. Every year we participate in an "Interline luncheon" for retired Flight Attendants in Southwest Florida. This luncheon is open to all retired airline Flight Attendants, from all airlines. In 2015, 139 enjoyed lunch together at the Naples Yacht Club. This year there were over 200.

My Kiwi group knows that I am writing my stories and the President of our Chapter asked me to read one of my chapters at a meeting. I read about flying on the new Boeing 747.

They all whooped and laughed and remembered many details right along with me...broken "elevators," parade of carts during the service. We had to walk "uphill" in the aisles.

Well, right there over lunch, with 16 retired birds, I asked about their first trip: "Did anyone put you in the overhead rack?!"

SQUEALS! "YES!! OH! YES!!"

Each one had gone through the initiation with the rest of the crew standing back to watch her climbing down...Oh, the laughter!!

Except two...in our Chapter. They were too tall for a cockpit crew member to put her in the overhead rack. These two Stewardesses, on their first trips, one in 1964 and the other in 1965, both based in Boston, just before the passengers boarded, were called up to the cockpit to have a "heart exam."

The "heart exam" was given by the Flight Engineer in the cockpit.

The Flight Engineer, the new, younger pilot who was going to work his way up to Co-Pilot, then Captain, had a piece of equipment that could be plugged in to a spot on the engineers' panel in the 727 or 707. This gadget had a long wire attached. So, with the Captain and Co-Pilot in place, getting ready to start their check-list, and a secret smile on their faces, the Engineer in his seat started flipping switches. This wide-eyed stewardess on her first trip sat still on the cockpit jumpseat while the Flight Engineer put this instrument down the front of her fly-boy collar (deep-v neckline) and moved it around for her "heart test."

The cockpit door was open for the other Stewardesses to watch and then laugh with the cockpit crew as she passed her "initiation."

I want to note here that this was back in the days before women were vocal about sexual harassment. We considered this all in good fun, innocent. It didn't feel sexist or demeaning. Once we passed our initiation we enjoyed watching and being in on the next "new stew's" initiation.

This all stopped when American hired men as Flight Attendants.

Our Kiwi group, at this same lunch, laughed about another detail during the "good ole days." Long Black Socks.

When we started flying in 1965, business men dressed up. The men wore long-sleeve dress shirts with a coat and tie. We even had a coat closet! We hung up sports jackets and suit coats as our first procedure.

But the real indication of a highly successful business man was his long black socks. Short black socks when you could see his ankle or leg wouldn't do.

Long Black Socks, and you thought we were checking seat belts...

Florida Suncoast Kiwi Chapter Honoring 9/11 Firefighters from New York City in Ft. Myers Beach, Florida

Short Stories

Captain Mitchell, Sir

There are several short stories that don't warrant a whole chapter, but I can't leave them out, these stories don't have anything to do with each other and the stories may be out of order in time.

I introduced myself to the Captain in Dallas in preparation for a domestic trip to New York. When I said that, "I am Tina Florer and our crew is from Washington." The Captain said, "I am Captain Mitchell, Sir," or "Mitchie Darlin'." You decide.

It is interesting to note that my Dad gave W.W. Mitchell ("Mitchie Darlin'") a check ride years before on a trip that went from D.C. to Charleston, West Virginia, then on to Nashville and Memphis. My Dad, a CAA Inspector at the time, was on the trip also to check on some new "Nav Aids" (Navigation Aids) that had been installed on the ground. Pilots receive updated NOTAMS (Notice To Air Men) that must be inserted in their manuals to keep all of their required information up to date on the new "Nav Aids." NOTAMS are published every 28 days. Some of these Notices give information on controlled airspace that is not permitted for flight in "restricted areas" or "danger areas" like mountains or tall radio towers. Navigation Aids are compasses, charts, radio or light beacons, radar, automatic direction finder, and now GPS (Global Positioning System) from satellites to help navigation in aircraft. The list goes on and on and is always improving with computers and ATC (Air Traffic Control). There are Visual Flying Rules (VFR) and Instrument Flying Rules (IFR).

All to keep us safe while flying.

My Dad told me about his check ride when I told him about Captain Mitchell's introduction.

It is also interesting that Mitch's wife was the first national president of our Kiwi organization. Remember that retired American Airlines Flight Attendants are "Kiwis" birds that don't fly.

I guess she called him "Mitchie Darlin."

Which is Which?

Years ago, before we started using a cart to serve beverages, we asked the passengers individually, row by row, what they would like to have and gave them choices of Coca Cola, 7-UP, orange juice, tomato juice, ginger ale, or water. We delivered their preferences from a tray, and then asked the next row or across the aisle what they would like to drink.

When the flying time was longer and the lunch or dinner service was finished an hour or two before, we needed to serve beverages again. This time we offered drinks from a tray with several choices on the tray: Coke, orange juice, or 7-UP. Passengers asked which one is the Coke? Picture the tray: Coke, orange juice, or 7-UP, they asked which one is the Coke?

We Flight Attendants were astounded at how often passengers asked which drink was which? We have asked Flight Attendants from other airlines about this and they heard the same question: which one is the Coke (or orange juice or 7-UP)?

At our Kiwi meetings, we have talked and laughed about this old memory and about how times have changed.

Acceptance Policy

Passenger acceptance policy:

Yes, there is such a thing. It is written by the government and airlines.

I know the old policy, but I looked on-line to see how things have changed and discovered that some of the old policies are still in place.

Passengers not accepted on the airplane, the old policy:

drunk
open toed shoes/flip flops
smell bad
ugly

Ugly? We may not realize it, but we are more tolerant than we used to be. This old acceptance rule was in place because of afflictions some people had and passengers didn't want to sit next to them. I wonder: Who was the judge out in the gate area before boarding? I have an example of how it was handled. On my domestic flight, years ago (before1980), a teenager traveling with her Mom had boils or some disease all over her face and neck, and they were oozing. This wasn't just acne, this was horrible, and hard to look at. The agent accepted her/them and put them in the front row of First Class, with the girl by the window and she faced the window the whole trip without being told. Please note: The front row of First Class is not a hiding place, neither is the front row of coach. Ugly is one rule that has been changed.

New Rules:

Drunk. A person who is visibly drunk is still not accepted on board.

Shoes. The new rule is that anyone older than five cannot be barefooted.

Smells bad: This rule is still in place. Again, I wonder who is judging?

Clothing that has offensive language on it: A rule that is new to me. If that person has a jacket to cover it up or changes clothes, he or she will be accepted. In my research, I found that Australia reported a passenger with a shirt that had the "f" word all over it and he wouldn't cover it up or change his shirt. He was not accepted on that flight.

Times have changed.

Our Song in Tune

American flies to Frankfurt, Germany from several cities in the U.S. The flights leave the different cities around the same time to arrive in Germany in the late morning. The routine is the airplane is on the ground for a couple of hours in time to be cleaned and catered before a new crew and passengers board to fly back across the Atlantic.

While I was flying to Frankfurt out of Miami, we stayed in Mainz which is about thirty-five minutes from the Frankfurt airport. We stayed at a beautiful hotel on the Rhine River, that is, all the crews stayed at the same hotel in Mainz. I loved staying in Mainz, it was historic and there were great restaurants nearby.

On this occasion, our crew shared the limo (van) to the airport with another crew, it was a big van with two crews, about twenty-eight crew members, twenty of which were Flight Attendants.

Someone started singing, "Cry Me a River." Then we all chimed in. Picture this, twenty women singing "Cry me a river" all the way to the airport.

Funny how we knew the words.

Handheld Devices

Now picture our world back in the days before any hand-held devices. We almost can't picture it. Young people today would call it the dark ages.

On this DC-10 with a full load, I was 1st Flight Attendant working in First Class. After the meal service, I noticed some men in coach standing up. They seemed to be looking over the shoulder of a man sitting on the aisle. Three men, then another man joined this group looking at something the seated man was holding in his hand. The man seemed to be explaining this device.

These men sat down as we began our descent to land.

I think this trip was from Dallas to Chicago. The next leg of our trip was from Chicago to Los Angeles and the same thing happened, after the meal service several men gathered around a seated man explaining a device he was holding. It was so weird.

The next week after a few days off there were several groups gathered throughout the airplane in coach and one group in First Class. And, the next week, no groups, our "long black socks" business passengers each had their own device: a Texas Instruments Calculator.

In June 1974, the United States Patent Office granted Texas Instruments the patent on this "miniature electronic calculator."

From our observation on board the airplane, this was the beginning of hand held wireless equipment that we now can't live without.

Several years later, a man sitting in First Class said to me that the airline that can provide (what we now call "Wi-Fi) in-flight connection for computers and cell phones will be the most successful airline.

That man was right, all the major airlines have full Wi-Fi capabilities, they have to, to keep up with the times and our young people.

A Blue Angel

In order to understand this event, you need to be able to picture the cockpit of a Blue Angel's F-4 Phantom airplane. The cockpit has tandem seats (one behind the other) and is about a man's shoulder width.

The "Blue Angels" is The U.S. Navy Flight Exhibition Team consisting of 16 officers, 110 enlisted with headquarters in Pensacola, Florida.

Formed in 1946, the Blue Angels started flying with the Grumman single propeller engine F6F-5 Hellcat. By 1967, they were flying the two jet engines McDonnell Douglas F-4J Phantom. Now they fly the McDonnell Douglas F/A-18 Hornet.

American Airlines has many former Navy and Marine pilots, but back in 1967 when the Captain told us that it was our new Flight Engineer's first flight as a civilian airline pilot we were excited, he was young and single! We didn't put him in the overhead rack in honor of his first trip, even when the Captain said he was a former pilot with the Blue Angels, but he was wide eyed as he boarded the airplane.

Before we started boarding the passengers, I asked our new pilot if he would like a cup of coffee. I will always remember the look on his face. He said yes and when I asked him how he likes his coffee, he just shook his head in amazement. I took him some coffee with cream.

During flight after we served the passengers lunch, I went up to the cockpit to apologize to the crew that I didn't have a choice of entrees to offer them, we only had chicken. The new Engineer burst out laughing, I guess there is no entree choice on the F-4 either.

Brakes Released

It is a little known fact that Flight Attendants are not paid until the brakes are released and the airplane starts moving away from the gate.

Boarding passengers: Flight Attendants not paid. If a Flight Attendant helps someone put a bag in the overhead compartment, she or he is just doing it to be nice or to keep the boarding process running smoothly. Many F/As start preparing the galley for the service during boarding, they aren't paid for it.

When there is a delay or mechanical problem: even if the passengers are on board, the Flight Attendants are not paid until the brakes are released.

After the plane is moving and the First Flight Attendant starts the "Taxi away PA," the Flight Attendants begin the Oxygen mask demonstration and exit location highlights, they are paid flight time pay. The flight time pay is adjusted according to seniority and is substantially higher.

Note: Flight Attendants are paid "on duty time" from the time they sign-in an hour before departure. The "on duty time" is very small:

about $2.80 an hour for their duty day. When the passengers board they have earned close to $1.40.

One Less Bell to Answer

In July of 2002, I worked to Paris for the last time. Then I flew to Ma-drid for the rest of the year. I could still hold a better schedule with weekends off to Madrid than I could flying to Paris with my seniority.

I didn't have an official "last trip" and party. What worked out to be my last trip was to Madrid. On the return to Miami, the Captain made an announcement to the passengers that it was my last flight after 37 years.

The passengers clapped and shook my hand as they left the airplane in Miami. I handed in my paperwork to retire at the end of December.

Some new rules since 9/11 curtailed transfers to different bases. I was able to help a friend who was "stuck" in New York. We could "lateral" or trade bases with a Flight Attendant or Purser if both had the same qualifications.

We were both Pursers on international flights, qualified on the same aircraft types: Boeing 747, 767, 777, and Airbus A320. We were both up to date with our Emergency Procedure Training and Purser Training. She put the paperwork through so she could transfer to our Miami International base. I submitted my paperwork to a supervisor at our International base at JFK. It was the last week of December. I retired December 31, 2002 out of Kennedy without flying a trip.

The Engineer

Bill fought several forms of cancer of the head and neck for twenty years, then died July 27, 2013. We did take dream-come-true cruises and adventures. We even flew back to Belfast, Northern Ireland and Scotland a couple of times to visit Bill's relatives. But during his third trip to the Mayo Clinic in Rochester, Minnesota, in February, 2013, he said, "That's it. I give. No more tests, no more treatments." While we were there they implanted a feeding tube and a permanent catheter.

He was such an Engineer, he thought about and perhaps worried about how I would do without him.

He died July 27th, my birthday was August 19.
He sent me flowers and a card.
Our 39th anniversary was November 30.
He sent me flowers and a card.
The flowers were from Heaven Scent Flowers in Bonita Springs.
December of 2012 we had our picture taken in front of our Christmas tree, he had it enlarged and framed, sent it to my brother in Virginia to give to me at Christmas.

Taxes:
My Mother died May 3, 2013, two months before Bill. In February

2014, I did my Mother's taxes for the last time. I didn't do them, I put everything in piles then gave them to the tax lady to prepare them.

In March around St. Patrick's Day I started to work on our taxes for 2013, as I went through our file of paperwork there was a page of Irish jokes, another page of Irish jokes, and a third page of Irish jokes.

I can hear him say, "I'm an Engineer you know."

A loving note: My Mother was in failing health in hospice, she was 91. I think she just stopped eating and died so that I could take care of Bill full time and not visit her every day. She is buried with my father at the Culpeper National Cemetery, next to the Flag Pole.

Culpeper National Cemetery Virginia

Sam, Tina, Stan with Grandma MiMi Watching the Matches,
Patty Took The Picture

Bill and Tina, Christmas 2012

"That's All"

As I sit here in contemplation after writing my stories about this incredible career, I see that life is a check ride. People are constantly observing you. Whether it is your boss or friends or family.

Observing, not judging.

I would be fortunate if all they observed in me, as my Buffalo supervisor noted on my first check ride, is that I have wispy hair.

Our passengers' observation and approval has made American Airlines successful since April 15, 1930.

We always have to remember no matter who is on board:

"It's Always a Check Ride"

Thank You

This could be a one-person page: Jim Robison. His encouragement as Professor of my collaborative writing class at Florida Gulf Coast University's Renaissance Academy has made me feel that my stories matter in history and information.

My brother, Stan, and his wife, Patty, have continued to be enthusiastic and kept me to my theme on the airplane.

Dick and Mary Paulson helped me with details in the cockpit and in training.

DaRuMa Japanese Steakhouse in Naples confirmed that the Japanese Tea Ceremony is correct.

Donna Lothian, my friend and tennis pal was the first to read these chapters to completion. She has been an encouraging sounding-board and her background as a teacher pushed me in the right direction.

Neighbor Jim Moxley gave me computer technical advice that was invaluable.

Joe Ferro, my dear friend, egged me on… about the book!

My DAR Chapter asked me to be the program at a meeting to tell about my book before it was a book. So did my Kiwi Chapter and The Men's Club of Bonita Springs.

Early in this journey, having written only a few chapters, I gave them to my minister, Dr. Doug Pratt, of First Presbyterian Church of

Bonita Springs. Two weeks later, Doug's first question was: "Who is your audience?"

Before he asked me that, I think I was my audience. Writing my stories filled a void and gave me a purpose after Bill died. Then I woke up and realized Flight Attendants, Pilots, Military Veterans, and Boeing experienced these events with me. I am writing this for them.

I couldn't be more thankful.

About the Author

Tina was raised in Virginia by her parents: a Southern lady and a WWII pilot. Tina has a very busy life as she is Veteran Services Chairman of her DAR (Daughters of the American Revolution) Barefoot Beach Chapter, once a month meets with her Florida South Coast Kiwi Chapter (retired American Airline Flight Attendants, we're birds that don't fly).

She participates with the Gulf Coast Writer's Association, and EAA Chapter 1067 (Experimental Aircraft Association) at the Naples Airport and EAA Young Eagles (8 to 17 year olds get to experience flying in a single engine prop plane) Tina volunteers in the back ground.

She is a member of First Presbyterian Church of Bonita Springs and enjoys tennis, dancing and traveling to Cape Cod.